OF FISH AND MEN

OF FISH AND MEN

TALES OF A SCOTTISH FISHER

(REVISED AND EXPANDED)

DAVID C. WATSON

CUALANN PRESS

ISBN-10: 0-9544416-7-2
ISBN-13: 978-0-9544416-7-8

Second Edition September 2005
Revised and Expanded

British Library Cataloguing in Publication Data. A catalogue record of this book is available at the British Library.

Printed by Bell & Bain, Glasgow

Published by Cualann Press Limited, 6 Corpach Drive, Dunfermline, KY12 7XG Scotland
Tel/Fax +44 (0)1383 733724
Email: cualann@btinternet.com
Website: www.cualann.com

What is life?

It is the flash of sunlight on a kingfisher's back.

It is the dance of the mayfly over still,

evening waters.

It is the late summer mist drifting wraith-like

across the lake's surface in the quiet of dawn.

Dedication

For all those with priorities to juggle.
For the places we long to fish.
And the fish we long to catch.

Contents

Photographs

Dr David C. Watson was born in Edinburgh in 1958 and attended George Watson's College in Morningside. He graduated from Edinburgh University with a degree in Ecological Science and went on to complete a Ph.D. in Marine Ecology at Glasgow University. He now works on a major industrial site in North West of England where he is responsible for environmental compliance. Married with two sons, the extensive new material for this expanded version of Dr Watson's first highly acclaimed book, was written in the brief moments of calm between work and ferrying his sons to various out-of-school activities.

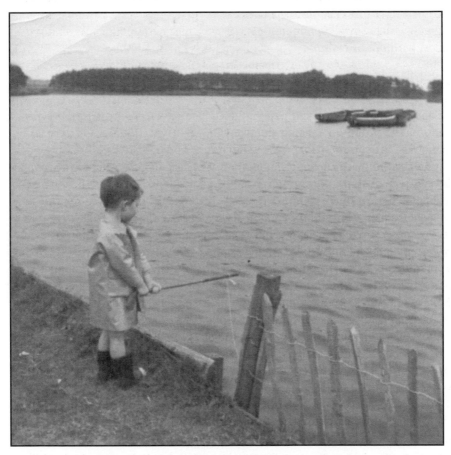

First fishing trip: golf club and string on Lanark Loch

Foreword

There have been many angling books written over the years instructing the reader on how to catch fish. Others recount the angler's exploits with monstrous fish on exotic and distant waters. All very well, and no doubt they enjoy a wide readership among the angling public. However, there is now a welcome return to the type of book where the author, an average sort of angler, recalls his or her experiences anecdotally, usually beginning with a nostalgic look back at early childhood with home-made rod and elementary tackle.

Anglers often identify with episodes which conjure up their own early days with rod and line. Feeling at one with the author, they are hooked for the remainder of the book. H. T. Sheringham and William Caine were such angling writers. One could imagine fishing with them and relaxing by the waterside at lunchtime with a leisurely flask of tea and sandwich while comparing notes on the morning's fishing.

David Watson follows in their footsteps in describing his angling life, 'Scrambling through a thicket of brambles, heedless of smarting scratches, he finally reached his goal: a magical, secret place where swirling waters quietened as they radiated out from beneath a towering waterfall.' We are at once on the same wavelength. How many of us can conjure up similar memories where everything in childhood is larger than real life? Even returning to that early scene as grown men and finding the fish smaller and the river no more than a stream cannot erase that youthful and enduring joy. David conveys this beautifully, just as he does the building of a bond between himself and his father as he anticipates his first fishing outing with the adults. 'Family life and all that went with it was at the centre of our existence, and it was only to be expected that we developed interests which, for many, became life-long bonds with our parents and maybe, in the future, will become so for our own children.' Such a bond is something we should all treasure but is, alas, a rare commodity nowadays in our brave new world. The author has been most fortunate in this respect and he realises his good fortune as he modestly describes his many encounters with Scottish trout in the company of first, his father, and then later, his wife, the latter being taught the gentle art while still his fiancée.

David is a modest angler and bravely admits to his having only ever caught one salmon, while the capture of a trout of over three pounds is still an achievement outstanding on his agenda. However, to my mind, he has the right attitude: 'I want to cover new water with every step, not knowing whether the next fish will be large or small, wondering what spectacle might greet my inquisitive gaze around the next corner. When I return from such a day, no matter the weather or catch, I return purged, temporarily at least, of the pressures and stresses of modern existence.'

With an honours degree in Ecological Science from Edinburgh University, David is well aware of the environmental hazards which threaten fish and their habitat, and, like all conservation-minded anglers, he treats his quarry with respect.

I thoroughly recommend this book to all those anglers who, like me, enjoy solitary fishing for trout of modest size in wild places, a world away from the small angler-crowded stock ponds and their unnaturally large hatchery fish.

Derek Mills
Melrose
Scotland

Introduction

How did I come to pen the first version of this book? Was it my love of writing and the peculiar satisfaction I have always derived from the carefully crafted word? Was it a desire to pass on to others some small measure of the joy fishing has given to me? Or was it just some deep-seated urge to escape from the grind of a career in remission and all the struggles associated with the daily business of survival?

Whatever the answer, it was not until I started looking back through the years of faded records and unlocking the memories stored in the dim recesses of my own mind that the true adventure of fishing became apparent to me. After the first words, the memories tumbled forth giving almost as much pleasure in the writing as they did in the living.

Writing and fishing have much in common. Both are, in their own ways, a search for perfection. The perfect cast, the perfect turn of phrase. In both, there is an element of obsession. The pen is no more readily stilled than the rod laid aside.

Sometimes, I catch myself day-dreaming of a veranda with panoramic views across the mountain wilds. Days spent casting a fly across majestic, rolling rivers, Brad Pitt-like in the summer sun. Evenings watching ideas take shape to the gentle clack of the keyboard, while the sun sets over the forests and the moths clamour around the swaying storm lantern.

Unfortunately, dream and reality are frequently very different sides of the same coin. A shrewd literary agent warned me a very long time ago that only the famous footballer, the pop star, the disgraced politician and the mass murderer make a living from writing. For a variety of reasons (including two left feet and a complete inability to pitch my voice) I am unlikely to achieve any of the foregoing, though there have been occasions in my day job, when the last seemed more than a faint possibility.

So I find myself here, not for the first time, in the dingy carriage of a West Coast express, running half an hour late somewhere between Warrington and Wigan, dreaming of fishing while the briefing notes for my meeting languish undisturbed on the coffee-stained formica top in front of me. Yet, as ever, life has moved on and there have been new experiences. Finding the perfect word to describe them is as much a challenge as catching the silvery trout that leaps in an iridescent shower of droplets at the tail of the pool. I can no more decline the challenge than stop breathing.

As Izaak Walton said, 'In writing of it I have made myself a recreation of a recreation.' Who am I to argue?

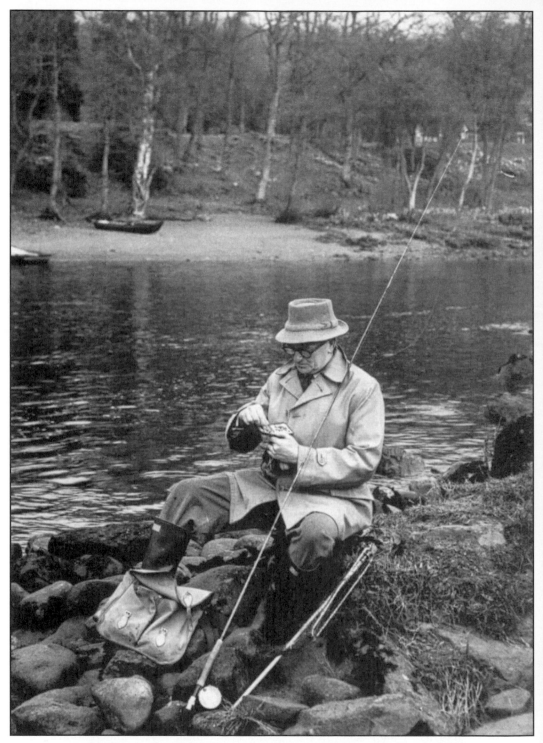

Fishing in the blood: the author's Great Uncle on the Tay in 1955

PART I
IN THE BEGINNING

I grew up in Morningside, that quirky enclave of Edinburgh life characterised by leafy sandstone terraces, well-to-do spinsters and blazer-clad schoolboys. As different to the nearby housing estates of Pilton or the industrial heartlands of Paisley, Motherwell and Kilmarnock as chalk from cheese, yet as implicitly and unreservedly Scottish as any.

As a child, my daily chore was doing the 'messages' at the local corner shop. 'Twenty Capstan and a pint of milk please, mister.' The immigrant community had yet to spot the potential for such establishments and out-of-town shopping was no more than a glint in some youthfully anonymous town planner's eye. The proprietor (universally known as 'open aw day') was a part of the community; you knew his name and he knew yours. Just one small manifestation of a bigger truth: we had identity; we belonged; life was safe and we knew every back street and every garden shed on our patch.

Family life and all that went with it was at the centre of our existence, and it was only to be expected that we developed interests which, for many, became life-long bonds with our parents and maybe in the future, will become so for our own children.

1

SENTENCED TO FISH

Through the window, Skye's beautiful and rugged scenery bounced by. The Cuillin ridge threw jagged spikes skyward, peaks etched in fine detail against the backdrop of white cloud piled up to the north. Momentarily visible over the lip of the cliff, the loch sparkled in the sunlight far below. By its banks sat the hunting lodge, our destination, its air of aloof austerity striking an incongruously sombre note on such a day.

But poetry and peaceful reflection were far from my mind. Instead, my eyes, indeed my whole being was trained on the small section of rough track visible through the mud spattered windscreen of the Landrover. The vehicle careered around another hairpin, stones scattering to right and left, the more energetic reaching the precipice and disappearing soundlessly into the void below.

To the left of my field of vision sat my father, rigid with fear, visage pale and knuckles white. To the right, the major hunched over the wheel, colour high, jaw jutting challengingly. For a second, in my imagination, the dashboard was the instrument panel of a Centurion tank and the major's worn Barbour jacket was starched military khaki.

To him, this was a challenge, a chance to prove that he could still live life close to the edge and defeat the odds, a chance to throw off the shackles of a cosseted existence and once more savour the thrill of combat. Only this time the enemy was the terrain, the weapon, a clapped out old Landrover and the likely casualties, my father and I.

Briefly, my stomach parted company with the rest of my digestive tract as all four wheels left the track simultaneously. Then my spine jarred as we returned to earth.

I gave in and simply shut my eyes to await our fate.

The family spent most summer holidays on Skye. We had grown to love the island in her gentler moods and to respect her when she donned her harsher face. Days of mist, wet clothes and frayed tempers all seemed worth suffering for just a glimpse of blue sky, of sunshine playing on the surface of the sea, eagles circling the crags and otters foraging playfully amongst the tangled kelp.

And for my father and me, of course, there was the fishing. Remote hill lochs, some familiar, others offering the excitement of secrets undiscovered. We lived for it, he and I, laying plans through the winter nights, poring over maps and rooting through fly boxes.

There was just one problem. The rest of the family did not fish. In fact, the rest of the family did not have even the most fleeting interest in fishing.

Which is why 'the river' was so tempting. Tumbling its short distance to the sea beneath the Bailey bridge, it was barely a mile from the cottage, within easy reach after the dishes had been washed and the breakfast table laid. We could fish that magical hour before dark and still be back by the time the last glow faded behind the ridge. At least we could have done, had the fishing not been private, as the stark new notice by the bridge proclaimed in no uncertain terms.

Like so much of the Scottish Highlands, the real riches of the land were the preserve of an absentee landlord, in this case, an ex-army man from the Borders rumoured to possess a fiery temper.

Our initial forays were brief, heart-thumping affairs. Caution was the watchword, one eye on the road, one on the water. Sneaking through the heather, rods assembled only when out of range of prying binoculars. But later, back in the warmth of the cottage with a brace of sleek little finnock on the slab, feelings of guilt were far from our minds.

And with time, the caution turned to brazenness. Was this not our home, our land to tramp, ours to fish when we pleased?

So one fine evening with the water running off after several days' rain and with expectation in my heart, I found myself, almost unawares, casting carefully across the bridge pool itself. My tail fly was just reaching that spot under the far bank where a finnock had splashed merrily moments before. My concentration was absolute, my whole world contained in that little eddy of water by the bank.

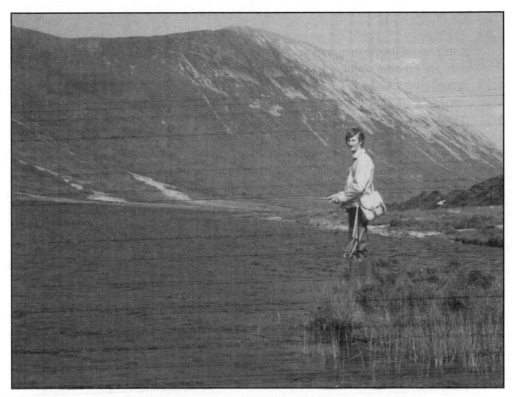

Fishing Sguabaidh where the river tumbles seawards

Then suddenly, without warning, some sixth sense told me that all was not as it should be. Concentration fled, the moment was lost, and my quarry hurtled across the pool like a silver missile leaving a v-wake on the oily surface of the shallows. I jerked upright from my half-crouch in exasperation and whipped around to confront a face, scant inches from mine.

Instantly, annoyance turned to panic. The owner of the face had the upright bearing of a man who was not accustomed to argument. I took in the plus-fours and tweed jacket, the beetling eyebrows and handlebar moustache in less time than it took to draw breath. For perhaps the first time in my young life I knew the taste of fear. I did not need to guess who had interrupted my sport.

For what seemed a lifetime, we stared at one another, frozen in a tableau of immobility. I could almost touch the deep, brooding wrath boiling ever closer to the surface. Like a rabbit caught in the glare of headlights, instinct told me I was lost if I did not move soon. For an instant, I broke eye contact and glanced down the river towards the sea pool where my father was casting, blissfully unaware of the peril close at hand.

This was no time for bravery, words tumbled over themselves as I rushed to shift the blame. It was his idea, he had suggested that we fish here, he was in charge …

Now my father was always an enthusiastic fisher. But his enthusiasm stemmed from the simple pleasures of countryside and companionship, peace and tranquillity. Not for him the difficult decision between Dog Nobbler and Booby, Peter Ross and Kingfisher Butcher. Deep discussions on the mating habits of the American brook trout were never the stuff of bank-side musings when he was your companion. Give him three wet flies and a nice bit of river; that was all he ever asked for.

However, crisis often breeds invention. And what crisis could be greater than this? The peace suddenly shattered by a lumbering figure, red with exertion, arms flailing like an out-of-control combine harvester, moustache twitching, spluttering and fuming from peak of deerstalker to tip of brogues. Visions of handcuffs, courtrooms and disapproving judges, all must have flashed before my father's eyes in that instant.

Yet faced with adversity, the human mind is often surprising in its capacity for clarity. Somewhere, sometime deep in the past, in an idle moment, my father had picked up a book on fishing, one of these serious tomes which talks of learned subjects like the changing pattern of salmon runs, the relative merits of brown trout and rainbows, and, yes, the legal niceties of fishing for that rarest denizen of the large estuary, that half sea trout, half brown trout, the slob trout. Suddenly, a wild glint of hope. Is the

slob trout not legally exempt from 'ownership'? Is it not the property of the common man?

Without hesitation, into that moment of stillness as one tirade gave way to the next, my father dropped his pearl, 'Actually, we were only fishing for slob trout.'

For an age, the world held its breath. The tension was palpable. Red cheeks deepened to scarlet as if at the onset of apoplexy. And then, just as I felt I could stand the strain not a moment longer, the anger drained visibly from the great man's face. Miraculously, in its place, I detected what might have been approval, acceptance of the bold genius of the remark ... and perhaps also the germ of a devious plan.

The reply when it came was strangely muted, almost an afterthought issued from the depths of moustache, 'Slob trout, my arse!' muttered the Major.

That is why, some weeks later, we found ourselves here, beholden to the man, duty bound to accompany him, our presence just the weapon he needed. After all, bad heart or not, he did need exercise, and with two younger men to row and to carry his tackle, he would be in no danger of over exertion. There was no way out, we were his for the rest of the holiday.

And if the truth be known, it had seemed to us like a fair deal: the spectre of the local courthouse banished and replaced instead by long days on one of Skye's finest lochs.

Later, as we sat in the dim light of the lodge, sipping whisky from the proffered flask, I could have sworn that our host was growing younger and straighter, that the lines were disappearing from his face as he spoke ... or was it just the whisky blurring my vision?

Loch Slapin and the Red Cuillins

2

HOOKED!

Tousled hair flopped above intent features as the boy strode purposefully through knee-high pasture, uncut since last summer. Buttercups and cornflowers nodded in his wake, swathes of parted grass closed slowly to mark his passage.

Through the stone circle which gave the cottage its name: no time to marvel at the red admiral startled from its sunny resting place amongst the

mosses and lichens. On past the damson trees, not a glance for the fruits ripening on heavy branches. And finally to the barbed wire which marked the perimeter of the field and the beginning of forbidden territory.

Relinquishing rod and bait tin, the boy ducked low and climbed swiftly between the strands. Catching the elbow of woollen jumper, he halted momentarily to tug the garment free, leaving the beginnings of a hole which would need repair.

Hurriedly, he retrieved his burdens and started along the overgrown and, in places, dangerously eroded bank of the little burn rushing impatiently towards Loch Earn. The undergrowth was lush now, growing tall around the decaying, moss-draped remains of trees long since dead. Above, mature beeches filtered the gentle sunlight, creating a delicate dappled effect on the ground. Errant sunbeams played mischievously on the water's surface as the burn ran merrily on across a bed of pebbles. Over its surface, mayfly and olives danced their time-honoured rituals undisturbed by the boy's noisy passage.

Scrambling through a thicket of brambles, heedless of smarting scratches, he finally reached his goal: a magical, secret place where swirling waters quietened as they radiated out from beneath a towering waterfall. A fallen tree spanned the middle of the pool, forming a narrow bridge, precarious but enticing. In a flash of black and white, a dipper flitted by, intent on its own business, ignoring the boy struggling in his haste to extend the little telescopic rod.

With practised fingers and urgent expression, the boy extricated from the bait tin a wriggling earthworm, fat from an easy life on the pasture. Fingers trembling, he threaded the worm onto the hook, hesitating now for just a moment to muster his courage. Then, gripping the rod between clenched teeth, he began to shin slowly out along the tree trunk until eventually he clung precariously above the deepest part of the pool, knees and clothing streaked green with algae. Pushing tangled hair from brow, the boy squinted expectantly into the cool depths below.

His eyes did not adjust immediately to the sparkling light playing off the surface and for a long moment he saw nothing. But before disappointment could take hold, his rapidly sharpening vision registered a barely perceptible movement and finally he made out a familiar shape, broad tail wagging in welcome in the gentle current. The boy relaxed, the object of his desire was there, just as he had been the day before.

With thumping heart, the boy steadied himself and shifted slightly to grip the rough bark more firmly between scuffed knees. With one hand, he extended the rod ever so cautiously over the water, tip pointing towards the chaotic maelstrom of froth beneath the waterfall.

Next, brow creased in concentration, the boy raised the worm-festooned hook in his free hand and swung it in a slow and deliberate arc out towards the current. With fine timing he let the rod tip drop just as the squirming mass reached the farthest point of its swing. With a plop only faintly audible above the roar of the falls, the bait landed where he had intended. The lead shot clamped to the nylon took hook and worm down quickly and out of sight.

For seconds that seemed to the waiting boy like hours, the bait trundled unhurriedly along the pebbly bottom. These moments were crucial; should another, smaller fish take the bait, the game would be up for today. Momentarily, the line stopped moving but a slight pressure was enough to dislodge the hook from some unseen snag.

Then, at last, it entered his field of vision, slowing now as the current eased. The boy could hardly bear to breathe. An eddy whisked the bait towards the fish's snout and time stood still altogether. With casual ease the fish flicked his great tail and moved forward leisurely to intercept the juicy morsel entering his territory. From above, the boy saw the momentary whiteness of the open mouth; then the bait disappeared.

All of the boy's intuitions told him to act but he knew better. With monumental self-control which belied his tender years, he waited until he sensed, rather than saw, the fish swallow. Seizing the moment, a sharp upward flick of the wrist struck the hook home.

Stung into action, the fish shot for the cover of the log. The boy was upright now, striving to hang on to his precarious perch and control the berserk thing thrashing below. In the limited confines of the pool, the fish fought with an alarming energy. For a while, it was all the boy could do to hang on. But slowly, oh so slowly, the tide began to turn. The runs were shorter, the tail thrashed with less vigour; the boy knew with certainty that the final hurdle was approaching.

Firmly, he drew the fish to the surface. From above, he could sense the laboured breathing and see the urgent fanning of the gills. Steeling himself, the boy swung his glittering prize out of the water and towards the bank in one smooth, practised movement. The little rod bent almost double with the strain and droplets of water scattered like confetti sparkling in the sunlight as they fell. Up over the bank the surprised fish flew, until it landed in deep grass far from danger.

Almost unable to contain himself, the boy scrambled back along the trunk, heedless of skinned knees as great chunks of bark and moss were dislodged to drift downstream like a flotilla of tiny ships. In seconds, he was on the bank and searching for his reward, impatient to claim what was rightfully his. When at last he found it, he knelt still for a long moment, beset by an unexpected pang of remorse. Then almost as quickly, pride took over.

Striding back through the pasture bearing his prize, the boy's thoughts, as a child's are apt to be, were all for the present. He was unaware that nothing would ever be the same again; unaware that, as the years passed and life became tarnished by experience, he would always have a way to escape, to recapture those same youthful feelings of joy and excitement. Had he known, he might have felt privileged.

Intense concentration: Loch Voil, 1968

ivious to the weather: Loch Morar, 1966

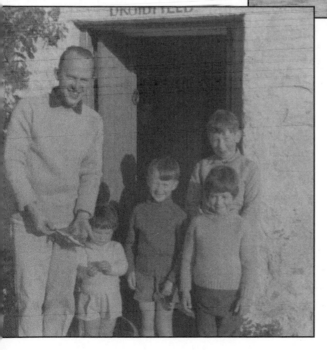

One for breakfast from the burn

3

A CHANCE LOST

It was not long until I got my eagerly awaited chance to fish with the menfolk. This august body included my father and would meet in the evening, laden with tackle and torchlights to fish through dusk and beyond on the big loch itself.

Their favourite haunt was a sheltered, sandy bay on the south shore. The trick was to wade across the shallows and fish where the bottom fell sharply away. Here, larger than average trout would root amongst the weed beds and follow the rising nymphs to the surface to gorge with uncharacteristic abandon as the light faded.

In retrospect, I have to say that my father and his cronies were not too fussy about how they caught their fish. Wet flies were, as often as not, adorned with squirming maggots, a lethal combination on the right night. Many mornings I had woken in the first light, clambered down the ladders from the primitive little loft with its shaky camp bed, padded barefoot across the cold stone floor to the kitchen to peer in awe at the previous night's catch lying on the slab by the sink, sometimes arranged for effect on a bed of fresh bracken leaves. There was nothing I wanted more than to join these forays, be a part of the excitement, share in the camaraderie of the night and in the glory of the morning after.

And then one day, over breakfast around the rough wooden table, my father had remarked to no one in particular, that he might take me along with him that evening. Buttered toast froze half way to my mouth. Even now, I can still feel the weight of tension which engulfed me as my mother considered her response. Just as I felt sure my heart would stop, she looked up from her plate, seemingly satisfied with her decision: I could go.

The rest of the day passed in a blur of anticipation. We took the womenfolk shopping, a necessary, time-honoured sacrifice. My father and I sat together in the front of the old Morris 1000 Traveller (father with patience born of long experience, son barely able to stop fidgeting) while the ladies explored the woollen mills and gift shops of nearby Comrie. My mother knew the rules of the game and knew just how far the credit of an evening's fishing extended.

Later, while father donned boots and slogged through brambles and nettles to clear a blockage in the water tank high on the hill behind the cottage, son did his penance too, tidying dinner dishes and setting the kitchen table in readiness for the following morning. The sun was low now and I knew the waiting was nearly over. Excitement mounting, I tore around the tiny cottage as if possessed, responding instantaneously to my mother's every command. Even my younger sister's mischievous attempts to divert me from my tasks were to no avail. Sulking, she wandered outside to play on her own.

Because Druidfield stood at the top of a quiet, unlit lane with no near neighbours, my mother would not leave the refuge of the cottage after dark. So my final chore was to take the empty milk bottles down the path to the little picket gate at the foot of the garden for the milkman to collect on his delivery round the following morning. I knew my father had the tackle in the car now and I could see him testing the storm lamp, impatient to be on his way. Two trips, I decided, were one too many. I gripped one bottle in each hand and pressed the remaining two to my breast.

Thus armed, I took off down the path as if the devil himself was on my tail, ignoring exhortations from the kitchen window to be careful. To any onlooker, what happened next must have seemed inevitable, the only surprise being how near I got to my goal before disaster struck. What caused me to tumble I do not know, but fall I did, right on top of the bottle clutched in my right hand. In an instant, blood sprayed everywhere, glass splinters glistening red where they protruded from slashed wrist.

Dropping storm lamp and duster simultaneously, my parents were there in seconds. Before I had time to gather my wits, I was bundled into the car, wrist wrapped in a dishtowel, bound for the doctor's surgery. As the car crunched over the gravel and onto the rutted lane, I uttered not a word. The pain shooting up my arm, even the threat of stitches, neither had any meaning. In the instant I fell, I had known that there would be no fishing that evening.

Long after the stitches healed, the scar would remain, a painful reminder of an opportunity missed and of companions betrayed.

A glimpse of Loch Earn: the big loch

4

THEN AND NOW

Looking back on childhood through the rose-tinted glasses of middle age, it is all too easy to see only perfection. Long, sunny, summer days guddling for trout in local streams or trotting worms down Highland burns. Crisp Edinburgh winters wading through snowdrifts on the way to school, pelting full tilt at treacherous ice slides on back-street pavements. Running free, in a world and an age when our parents had no need to be concerned about what would become of us. We knew our neighbours. They knew us. We looked out for each other.

I have to search hard in the recesses of my mind to recall the frustration and frayed tempers of confinement as the Skye rain drove mercilessly in from the sea, and the wind moaned and whistled in the scrub birch and pine that offered some shelter to the house. Or to remember the depression and discouragement of dour days on the hill lochs watching my father catch fish while I caught nothing. I have all but forgotten painful schoolboy memories of chapped legs and raw ears, shivering on some forlorn Edinburgh playing field, mud frozen hard by the bitterness of the wind, changing rooms stark and bare, taps leaking water hardly warmer than the frost-rimmed pool growing steadily under the uprights.

But one thing I remember with undiluted clarity is the irresistible fascination that water held for me. Lakes, streams and rock pools drew me towards them like a trout to a mayfly. In my quieter moments, all I wanted to do was peer into the shady depths and wonder at what they might contain. When I had energy to burn, I wanted to throw stones into them, jump across them or roll up my trouser legs and wade in them.

Fishing, as life, seemed simpler and somehow more accessible. There were the Lothian reservoirs, the Border streams, the association waters on the Tweed, the school beat, the lochs and burns of Skye whispering beguiling Gaelic names like Allt na Dunaiche, Rèidh nan Loch, Cuil na Creig and Lochan na Saile. Permits on the local waters were inexpensive and on the burns and lochs, unasked for.

Yet, there was a twist in the tale. The reservoirs were over-fished and under-stocked, catches were poor and dropping. On the Tweed, there was UDN, the scourge of salmon stocks for so many years. Sick fish twisted listlessly in the backwaters, a sad parody of their majestic selves. The Borders streams and rivers still suffered mightily from the damage inflicted during the industrial revolution, when captains of industry commissioned a network of insurmountable weirs, caulds and mill lades to guarantee power for their businesses and satisfy their entrepreneurial greed.

Across the water in Fife, Loch Leven, once famous for its unique and beautiful brown trout, suffered increasingly from the effects of industrial and agricultural pollution before regulatory control and public outrage became constraining forces. Catches dropped to an all time low and the water was abandoned in droves by those who had fished it for most of a lifetime.

Even the adaptable new kid on the block, the still-exotic rainbow trout, was proving a mixed blessing. Beguiled by its quick growth and adaptability, the new breed of fishery manager failed to understand (or chose to ignore) the limitations of the species in British waters and the complexities of its relationship with our native brown trout.

The result was over-stocked fisheries, poor quality, outsize fish, slimy and sluggish parodies of their wild relatives, and an obsession with bag limits, lures and lead core lines echoing the 'fast food', 'throw away' culture already just around the corner. An angling society that craved, above all else, size and quantity.

In the cold light of day, yesterday was neither better nor worse. Simply different.

Hill-loch brownies: a fine bag from Loch Sletill, Caithness

PART II
LEARNING THE ROPES

Schooldays, they say, are the best days of your life. Not really surprising, since they are the first days one remembers with any clarity and are, therefore, seen through the most strongly rose tinted glasses.

As befitted my Morningside upbringing, I joined the blazer-clad masses at a local private school where the standard of teaching, mercifully, was sufficiently high to instil in me some measure of pride in my academic performance (hitherto, seriously threatened by my love of sports, most specifically, football).

School, however, was not without its drawbacks. Prime amongst these was the painfully early introduction which a private education gives to the mind-numbingly stifling culture of the exam. Even through the haziness of time, I look back with a degree of sadness at long days spent closeted in my bedroom before Mock Highers, Highers and Certificates of Sixth Year Studies. At that age, life is altogether too precious.

The exclusively male atmosphere was another flaw which grew in importance as the years passed. When, in my last year, the fairer sex was finally admitted for the first time, we might just as well have been asked to communicate with aliens from another world. My abiding memory of that year (apart from the endless games of commonroom poker) was of the House Shakespeare competition, entered not to satisfy any limited thespian ambition, but rather, because extra-mural practice with a largely female cast was implicit. The psychological torture which ensued when I discovered that my role (Lysander in 'A Midsummer Night's Dream') entailed interaction of a faintly intimate nature was, I still maintain, the reason why I failed my CSYS Statistics ...

1

NO PAIN, NO GAIN

If ever a relationship could be described as 'love and hate' then my sporadic but nearly life-long dalliance with the king of fish, *salmo salar*, the mighty Atlantic salmon, is such.

My introduction to the joys and frustrations of angling for salmon came when I was still a schoolboy of tender years. The school had been bequeathed the fishing rights on a productive stretch of the River Tweed, that east coast river famed in recent decades for its prolific autumn fishing. The deal was that parents and teachers could fish the river but only if accompanying pupils, or at least such was the theory. Sadly, there was a tendency for certain amongst the former to see this as a convenient meal ticket to fishing normally beyond their means. Notwithstanding, it still presented a marvellous opportunity for youngsters to learn at an early age the joys and privileges of a pastime which would remain with them throughout their lives.

The main run of fish in these days was getting later by the year, indeed, it was often well into November before catches began to rise. Unfortunately, the weather on the east coast of Scotland at that time of year can be unforgiving. My most enduring memories of Tweed days are of fingers and toes past the point of pain after hours up to my chest in the Boat Pool or the Gleddis Weel amidst swirling, near-freezing waters fresh from snow-covered moors. Sometimes, the first tentative step off the bank would be greeted by the crack of splintering ice. On such days, it was often necessary to stop periodically to breathe over rod rings frozen by the autumn hoar.

The compensation, of course, was the sheer dazzling beauty of the early morning, the delicate tracery of spiders' webs heavy with frost and sparkling in the sunlight amongst the undergrowth, the sharp freshness of the air on each intake of breath. And then there was the camaraderie as teachers, pupils and parents alike set forth with high spirits and anticipation. And finally, at the end of the day, the glow that came after the pain of thawing hands and feet.

All these pleasures I shared with my fellow anglers. However, the ultimate pleasure, catching a salmon, was denied to me for what seemed an interminably long time. I saw salmon, often at close quarters as I stepped into the river, and a monstrous silver form shot from under my very feet. I saw other people catch salmon: most notably my maths teacher, whose main tactic seemed to be sheer, heroic perseverance. When I arrived in the morning, he would be there, standing up to his chest in that beautiful run by the hut, like some great and patient heron and he would be there still as I made my way back to the car park in the autumn gloaming.

Then one day, all unsuspected, my luck changed. The day began no differently to any other. There was a good stock of fish in the beat, as evidenced by the occasional exuberant splash half way up the Boat Pool where the run dissipated into the body of slower moving water. I had already fished down the pool once. My father was sitting on the bank attacking the lunch box and Mr Doull, the soft-spoken English master, was working his quiet way down the pool below me.

My mind was pretty much in neutral; secretly I had stopped believing that I could ever actually catch a salmon, a state of mind in which I felt quite comfortable, bereft of any real sense of expectation. Instead, I concentrated on the aesthetic pleasures of casting. With such a philosophy, I had discovered, I was no longer disappointed and frustrated, just content to be spending a day in the open air doing something I enjoyed doing.

So when my size six Thunder and Lightning stopped half way round its gentle arc across the streaming water, I naturally assumed that it was more weed, dislodged by last week's rain and drifting on its leisurely way down the river, the last reminder of a summer now long since past. But then the 'weed' started to move rather faster than weed is apt to do, my reel screamed, and line whipped uncontrolled through the rings of the big double-handed rod. Suddenly, my cosy state of self-induced catatonia was interrupted with a start.

Unfortunately, I had generally considered lessons on what to do after the salmon was hooked to be of academic interest only. My father, who was on his feet by this time, sandwiches forgotten, was as much a novice as I was and no coherent advice was likely to come from that quarter. Further down river, Mr Doull was as yet unaware of the momentous happenings upstream. I was on my own. I had waited a long time for this moment and suffered much pain along the way. Cool determination took over. I was not about to fail now.

Surviving on a wing and a prayer at first but gaining in confidence as the minutes passed, I stopped letting the fish play me and began gingerly to take control. Gradually, the frenzied runs got shorter and the leaps less prodigious. For the first time, I got a really clear view of my quarry. His sheer size took my breath away. By now, Mr Doull had joined my father on the bank and was supplying advice in a calm, no-nonsense manner.

It was now nearly a quarter of an hour since my own fortunes and that of my first salmon had become irretrievably entwined. The point was rapidly approaching where I would have to take some action to end the struggle. Mr Doull was a step ahead of me. Following his instructions, my father had already entered the water, jaw set in a firm line of determination. This was unknown territory for him too.

Calling on the last of my dwindling strength, I drew the fish towards his outstretched hands. Like a pro, he timed his lunge to perfection and the salmon, too tired to protest, yielded to his firm grip. Onto the bank it was heaved and suddenly the tension was broken. In an instant I found myself submerged beneath back slaps and handshakes. It was like a dream, the impossible had happened. I had caught my first salmon. I was a salmon angler.

Life, however, has a habit of biting back.

It is now more than thirty years since that autumn day and I have caught not a single, solitary salmon since. In my defence, my salmon fishing has been sporadic, a day grabbed here and another there with perhaps seasons intervening. However, the list of waters with which I am acquainted reads like a roll call of the very finest salmon waters in the British Isles: the Tweed, the Tummel, the Aberdeenshire Don, the Laxdale, the Tay, the Thurso, the Annan, and, most recently, the Erriff and Cashla in western Ireland. I have fished on rivers so stiff with salmon that I could have walked from one bank to another without so much as getting my feet wet. But although I have enjoyed fishing each and every one of them, I have still failed to catch another salmon.

And yet, untainted by the disappointments which have followed, that autumn day on the mighty Tweed remains for ever etched on my memory. No fading photo is required to remind me of that salmon's silvery flanks, or of the mixed feelings of elation, respect and sadness as it lay on the bank, finally defeated in its efforts to reach the spawning grounds of its birth.

Perhaps secretly, somewhere in my subconscious, I have felt since that to catch another of its noble brethren would in some way detract from the wondrous memory of that moment. Or then again, perhaps I am just a hopeless salmon fisher.

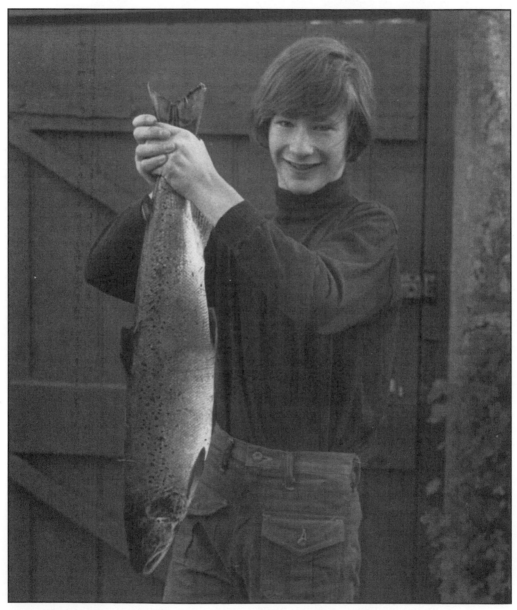

That first salmon: River Tweed, 1973

2

FORBIDDEN FRUITS

That much-travelled fishing writer, John Gierach, once compared fishing to sex. Although in my experience, one generally lasts longer and comes along more frequently than the other, the comparison, nevertheless, was an astute one. Like sex, the more forbidden and less accessible the fishing, the more enticing it becomes. The bigger and bolder the prohibition notices, the more expensive the permit, the higher the fences, the more the rod arm is wont to twitch and the guiltier the thoughts become.

But like sex too, or so I am told, forbidden fishing is not necessarily good fishing or satisfying fishing. Looking back to years long past, my occasional forays uninvited on to premium waters protected by barbed wire ('I never saw the sign, honest Guv ... ') were never outstandingly successful. Perhaps the pangs of guilt transmit themselves down the fly line. Perhaps the fish recognised my humble origins and rumbled my fakery.

As I write, I am conscious of the outraged breath of the reader, hot on my neck, and the accusatory exclamations in my ear: 'Poacher!' I hear the word echo around the room. And if, in youthfully straying where by rights I should not, I was really guilty of a heinous crime, then I will lay down my rod and come quietly. But is not the real fishing rapist a different beast altogether? The criminal element, the organised gang that replaces fly with gelignite, poison or net, that takes vastly and cruelly, giving nothing back: the thug who will not stop short of violence to reap his grisly reward.

I have not had first-hand experience of such people. I have come close, though. Years ago, I spent a long, hot summer working on a trout farm by the lovely little Arle, a tiny chalk stream in deepest Hampshire. The beauty of the place, soft rolling farmland, sunny water meadows bedecked with wildflowers and buzzing with jewel-winged dragonflies, made a most incongruous setting for violence of any sort.

Yet my predecessor on the farm had left his job with two fingers fewer than when he started. A Landrover had driven up one dark and stormy night, the padlocked gates had been forced open with wire-cutters and the stock ponds bathed in the beam of searchlights.

The student had been living on the site in a tiny two-roomed mobile home, no doubt trying to earn a little money to supplement a meagre grant. Awoken by the sound of tyres on gravel and braver by far than I would have been, he had hastened to intercept the vehicle and challenge its occupants.

With stubborn determination, the young man had insisted on searching the back of the Landrover, no doubt expecting to find damning evidence there. By the light of torch he could hardly have failed to spot the damp sack strategically placed on the tailgate. His biggest mistake was asking to see what was inside. Helpfully, the driver had held the sack open for inspection. Plunging his hand into the dark depths, the student had expected to feel the clammy slime of dead fish. Instead, his hand entered the jaws of a primed gin trap.

There are many words suitable for describing such people but I would not wish to print any of them here. That is the truly evil side of poaching, as far removed from fishing as rape is from lovemaking. The perpetrators are criminals and despoilers of the worst sort and deserve to be reviled as such. They bear not even passing comparison to the wily old rogue after one for the pot and one to pass under the counter to the local hotelier ... or, I would argue, to the exuberant fisher weighed down by guilt and fly rod as he samples briefly of forbidden fruits.

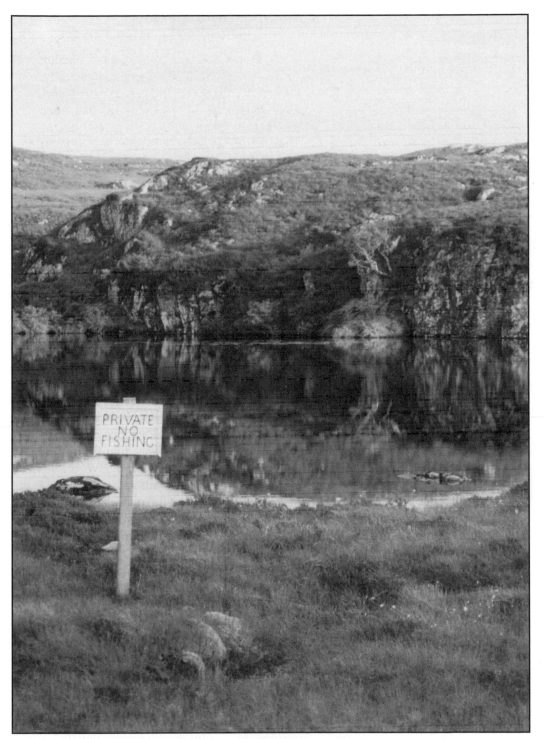

Temptation

3

FISHING, FASHION
AND THE FAIR SEX

During the seventies, I was a fairly frequent visitor to a popular but rather ugly fishery in the mining belt not far from Edinburgh. Those were the days when stocked fisheries were something of a novelty in Scotland and even hardened anglers thought of a 'rainbow' only as a natural phenomenon associated with sun, rain and a sizeable fortune. Because of its particular location, this fishery had rapidly become something of a meeting of cultures and fashions that, at best, typified the breadth of appeal which angling has and, at worst, threatened to erupt into open warfare (treble hooks at ten paces).

Lining up on one side of the car park, were the 'Jims' (as we knew them), stalwarts of the local mining community, no traditional straightjackets to constrain in any way their *modus operandi*. They were immediately recognisable in their gaudy yellow oilskins or sleeveless vests, cigarettes *de rigeur*, weight forward, fast sinking lines adorned with size 6 Baby Dolls, oozing foul language and loud conversation.

'Hey, Jimmie, ye catch anything yet?'

'No ******* chance, Jimmie, there's nay ******* fish in this loch!'

And on the other side, eyeing the opposition with disdain, were the 'Tweeds', positively bristling with deerstalkers, plus fours and pipes, split cane rods, floating lines and dry flies. To a man, they were solicitors and barristers up from Edinburgh on the office outing, entertaining clients or simply taking a break from Tweed, Spey or Dee: all with a lengthy, if often imaginary, tradition to uphold.

As you might surmise, there was little love lost between the two opposing factions. Though neither side would ever admit as much, I suspect that this was due more to the similarities than to the differences. The Jims derived enormous and undisguised pleasure cutting across the Tweeds' bows, outboards revved to maximum capacity, or anchoring up in the middle of the best wet fly drift, flaying the water mercilessly with heavy, lead-cored lines and cutting the surface to ribbons. The Tweeds, meantime, did not hesitate to drift across the lines of anchored Jims. Scant heed was paid to safety or unwritten code of conduct.

When that dreadful monstrosity, the Popping Bug, made a mercifully brief appearance on this side of the Atlantic, I remember only too well the gleeful manner with which the Jims took it to their hearts, rather, I suspect, for its trouble-making potential than any inherent ability to catch fish. Stripped through the water, looking more like a frog on jet skis than anything of natural birth, the popping bug prompted exchanges that I suspect were audible in Queensferry, clear across the Firth of Forth.

Of course, both clans were highly competitive: the Tweeds in a less overt manner, perhaps, quiet wagers changing hands in the boathouse to the accompaniment of conspiratorial whispers. A bottle of single malt, or a round of drinks at the club. The Jims, by contrast, collected the kitty with many a ribald remark on the pier. The score was communicated loudly from one boat to another in cheerful anticipation of a fine night down the boozers of Methyl or Dunfermline.

Female company was tolerated by both groups but was certainly not accorded any special privilege. I remember sitting in the car, warming my hands over a cup of coffee and looking out over fleck-capped waves late one season, while a not insignificant drama unfolded before my eyes. The stakes must have been unusually high because the Jims were deadly serious on this day. With them was one solitary woman.

As rivalry mounted, this lady was unfortunate enough to intercept an airborne Baby Doll. Whisked from its intended trajectory, no doubt, by an unusually violent squall, the fly embedded itself firmly in the lid of the luckless lady's right eye. The ensuing scream of outboard and churning bow wave were, I erroneously thought, designed to get her across the Road Bridge to the Edinburgh Royal Infirmary outpatients department with minimum delay.

However, as the boat ground to a halt on the gravel spit, the poor woman was shoved bodily over the side into the breaking waves. Before she had extricated herself from the churning froth, the outboard was whirring and her erstwhile companion was on his way, tying on a new Baby Doll as he went.

For my part, about the closest contact I had as a youngster with the fair sex through fishing (and even this is stretching the point somewhat) came on train trips separated by a couple of summers. The first time, I was travelling the West Highland line to Mallaig *en route* for Rhum. On the second occasion, I was on the opposite coast, heading for Forsinard and the magical trout lochs of the Caithness heather floes. (All of which, incidentally, just goes to prove how wrong you can be: clearly, all those single men who skulk on railway platforms the length and breadth of the country with little notepads and plastic lunch boxes are not there just to record the serial numbers of passing trains).

The girl I met on the way to Mallaig kept in touch for many years. The Forsinard trip was, in the end, less rewarding. My chances with the two delightfully blonde and blue-eyed German students unfortunate enough to end up in our compartment were not, I suspect, enhanced by the behaviour of my companion, who spent the entire journey hunched silently over a fly reel, winding the handle incessantly, in gleeful anticipation of the epic battles which he imagined to lie ahead. Occasionally, he would grunt with satisfaction and grin maniacally to himself. At Helmsdale station, my parting invitation to join us for a drink at the fishing hotel was born of forlorn hope. Indeed, the two girls seemed at the time to disembark with wholly undue haste.

In nearly forty years of fishing, that is it. Or nearly it. There is just one other encounter that, for all its brevity, left a much more lasting mark on an impressionable mind. My handy little phrase book, *Norwegian for Every Occasion*, failed to live up to its promise the day I happened upon a young (but nonetheless notably well developed) Norwegian lady sunbathing nude by a little trout stream in Telemark. My Spey cast has never been the same since.

PART III

GROWING UP

The teen years represent a time for causes: a time for following one's heart, pursuing firmly held beliefs, a time before the hang-ups of maturity bring an overwhelming seriousness to life.

Being a teenager in early-seventies Scotland was about 'rollermania', that tartan be-decked Scottish manifestation of the frivolity which was a reaction to the depressing and sombre death throes of the sixties. It was about nationalism in the face of unashamed exploitation of the thick black oil pumped ashore on Scottish soil to Scottish cities. It was about a dawning realisation that humanity, despite the afterglow from the American moon landings, was not infallible and was probably not destined to live forever.

So we set forth in our frayed jeans and our cheesecloth shirts to save whales, creatures we had only seen (and perhaps that was the point) on TV documentaries. For every penny in the collection box we suffered slammed doors, profanities and misunderstanding. But we cherished every minute because life had meaning and purpose, and we were doing something our parents had never done and might never understand.

1

ONCE IN A LIFETIME

There are occasions, maybe only once or twice in a lifetime, when the most hardened cynic is left speechless with wonder, occasions which inspire poetry from the lips of the phlegmatic, leaving the poet at once enriched and melancholy for their passing.

My miracle happened one glorious summer's day when I was still in my early teens, not yet at the stage when family holidays had lost their appeal, but certainly with sufficient individuality to know what I wanted from my holiday and to be less than good company if I did not get it. What I wanted, and what I was not getting, was fishing.

Lost in black thoughts, I was moodily whacking at an innocent clump of bog cotton, hardly receptive to a miracle of whatever sort. High behind me the mighty Blaven reared, not the threatening, mist-shrouded hulk of the last few days, but showing instead a benign aspect, wet scree glistening in the sun, tooth-like crags etched in relief against a deep blue sky, smiling it seemed in defiance of my bleak mood. Below, Arinacraig was dwarfed, whitewash striking against the burgeoning purples of late summer heather. At the head of the glen, Loch Sguabaidh and the river seemed pocket-size, like traces on my father's tattered map.

Decapitating another imaginary enemy with bitter relish, my eye was caught briefly by a flash of silver. As I looked up, I was jerked abruptly from my introverted gloom, my breath taken away by the sheer magic of the scene unfolding far below. The seaweed-covered fringes of Loch Slapin, exposed by the ebbing tide, glittered like the treasure in some mythical goblin's cave. As I watched, the effect faded and then returned, rushing along the shoreline like a latter-day Mexican wave, until the entire loch seemed to be hung with a necklace of multi-faceted diamonds.

Gathering my numbed wits with an effort, I pelted down the hill towards the cottage, leaping from tussock to tussock, breath coming in snatches, seething clouds of adolescent gloom magically lifted. As I went, I yelled for the sheer joy of the moment just one word over and over: 'Mackerel! Mackerel!' Barely breaking my stride to grab the little rod propped against the wall of the cottage, I ran on, over the rutted single track road, across the field, scattering sheep to right and left, on over the boulders that marked the top of the shore, slowing only as I reached the first straggling outcrops of seaweed.

At last I had to stop, seawater slopped around the ankles of my boots, seeping through the luxuriant piles of bladderwrack. Looking around me, the scene that met my gaze bore no resemblance to reality. I felt like a prince in the royal treasury; around my feet and as far as the eye could see, the seaweed was ankle-deep with sparkling, silvery sprat, billion upon billion, driven onto the rocks by the massed ranks of their fellows piling ever shorewards. Beyond, hunting in packs, predatory mackerel leapt and cavorted, sating prodigious appetites on the easy pickings. Further out still, seals rolled lazily, feasting at their leisure.

I looked on in stunned awe for long minutes, the riot of colours transfixing me, blinding in its richness and intensity. Then I remembered why I was here: I too wanted a share in this bonanza.

Unhooking the little mepps spoon with fumbling fingers, I cast out into the seething molten silver. Almost before I had started to retrieve, the little rod bucked in my hands as a powerful mackerel took hold. Twice I repeated the act, twice more the rod kicked in triumph. Then, as suddenly as it had started, the silver shimmered like a desert mirage and faded out to sea, leaving behind its living debris piled high around my feet.

Out on the loch, the rowing boat from Faolin continued to catch fish for a little longer, then for it too, nothing stirred.

Each year thereafter, the little rod stood by the cottage door, waiting in eager anticipation. For a while, the occasional shoal did appear but never to fill the loch as far as the eye could see as it had that summer. And as the years rolled by, the shoals dwindled and came less frequently. For mackerel and sprat, linked since time immemorial as predator and prey, fate had dealt the same card: ruthless exploitation by the fishing fleets, soulless slaughter in nets of illegal mesh-size.

Yet their story is not unique: listen and hear the death song of the great whales as nations flaunt the International Whaling Commission's moratorium in the name of science; listen to the endless drone of drift net slipping over stern to plunder indiscriminately from the Greenland salmon fisheries.

For all the criticism that anglers sometimes receive, the greatest threats to our fish stocks and to our environment come from far more sinister quarters. But the angling fraternity is a powerful body; it is our obligation to use that power to act as guardians of a resource which provides us with riches beyond measure. We must be loud in our opposition to those who would despoil, if only for the sake of our children, so that they too can experience the miracles that put perspective on our increasingly sanitised existence.

Arinacraig, nestling at the foot of Blaven, Isle of Skye

Loch Slapin with Faolin just visible on the point

2

GOING SOLO

Like a first kiss, the first solo fishing outing is a pivotal event in an angler's life, opening up whole new horizons and possibilities previously undreamed of. And like the first kiss too, the first solo outing is apt to be planned to the very finest detail with that intoxicating mixture of excitement, anticipation and shy embarrassment.

Mine was to a little reservoir in East Lothian not far from the pretty town of Gifford, long popular amongst well-heeled, retired couples from nearby Edinburgh. The venue owed nothing to chance; on the contrary, it had been chosen with great care. Donnolly was only a short drive from my parents' home, the permit was inexpensive and the reservoir was sheltered from the blasting winds which could make Auld Reekie an inhospitable city and fishing in the Lothians a hazardous pastime.

It had taken long weeks and much patient scheming to win my parents round, due as much (leastways in my father's case) to borrowing the car as to the inherent dangers of boat fishing alone. By the time the appointed day arrived, I had already undertaken a dry run of the route and located the Water Board's offices where I would collect my permit. I was in a fair stew of excitement and had followed hourly weather bulletins with near religious fervour for several days.

As it happened, it was not the weather that let me down: it was the fish, or perhaps, more accurately, my ability to catch them. I arrived at Donnolly and pulled the car off the road with exaggerated care and not a little trepidation. Emerging from the trees at the water's edge, I found a light wind ruffling the surface. The sun was hidden behind a thick, but not threatening, layer of cloud. Conditions could barely have been better.

Out on the reservoir, an air of tranquillity descended as I drifted gently towards the dam. There was just the one solitary boat; bank fishing was not allowed. So I was alone, except, that is, for some mallard, a family of coot which dove from time to time at the very edge of my vision, looking alarmingly like rising fish, and an insomniac owl which hooted repeatedly when I least expected it, shattering the quiet and frightening the wits out of me.

Nothing showed by way of fish until early evening when a steady rise developed in the lee of the shore. Here, stately beech mingled with dainty birch crowded close to the water's edge, branches reaching out to caress the very surface. The fish were small, shy, wild trout and more than a match for me. They would come hurtling up from the crystal clear depths to take the tiny midge pupae barely visible in the surface film and then return as quickly to the safety of their hidden lairs, before I, in my relative inexperience, could react and cover the spreading rings.

But to be honest, none of that really mattered. What was important was the freedom, the solitude, the feeling of real independence which combined to make the day what it really was: the beginning of adulthood. A whole lifetime of experience beckoned and I resolved there and then to enjoy it to the full.

AT THE EDGE OF THE WORLD

Lazily, I opened my eyes and propped myself up on one elbow. To the west, the sea was an intense, endless expanse of azure blue. Already, the sun dipped low towards the horizon. On the ridge opposite, a solitary stag grazed apprehensively, raising his head occasionally to glance in my direction. Below me, Priomh Loch nestled peacefully, a gem in Rum's crown. The white lilies bedecking her quiet surface were half closed now, and the two divers had ceased their plaintive calls and settled for the night.

We were here to work for the Nature Conservancy Council, building bridges, mending roads and tending the Highland garrons (hardy ponies bred for carrying stags off the hills during the stalking season) that roamed the grassy swards by the shore. But, in truth, it was the hill lochs and the promise of free-rising trout that had brought us to this wild and remote place.

And all unawares, Rum, at once grand and quirky, island of contrasts, had ensnared me with her beauty. I had glimpsed the turrets of her castle, nestling in the magical depths of bluebell carpeted woods, I had watched wisps of mist swirl around rugged Hallival and Askival with their sheerwater colonies, and I had marvelled at the majesty of the sea eagles as they soared above the cliffs of Harris. This was Rum, a microcosm of Scotland itself.

I broke off from my musings and shifted slightly to look at the loch below. Idly, I noted that something had changed. But in my dreamy state of semi-consciousness it was some moments before the penny dropped. When it did, I jerked rapidly into complete wakefulness. Below me, the rhythm of my friend's casting had changed. To my tutored eye it seemed more frantic now, no longer languid and mechanical as before. Then I saw why. Off the headland, at the very edge of the lilies, concentric circles spread gently outwards across the mirror still surface.

With an audible swish, my friend's cast changed direction in mid-air and hit the water with a smack. I stifled the ghost of a grin. Undaunted, the gentle rise repeated itself, only this time a little further out along the lily bed, frustratingly beyond reach. As if by some invisible signal, another fish rose to the left, and then another ...

Belatedly, I realised that I was witnessing the beginnings of the evening rise. Galvanised from my lethargy, I was up in a moment and crashing through the knee-deep heather towards the water's edge on legs still stiff from rest. The stag, forgotten now, took off over the ridge in sudden panic.

Reaching the bank, I grabbed my rod, stripped off line and cast, unthinking, towards the nearest rise. But unsophisticated though they were, not even these naïve lochan trout were about to be fooled by a bushy size ten Soldier Palmer, a Dark Mackerel and a Silver Invicta retrieved like tiny torpedoes across a glassy surface.

Heart thumping and fingers trembling, I fumbled ineffectually with a reel of much lighter nylon. Stuffing the old cast unceremoniously into my bag, I managed on the third or fourth attempt to control my fingers sufficiently to tie the necessary knots. On went a size fourteen Light Olive and I was ready to go again.

Taking a deep breath and forcing myself to slow down, I spotted a gentle little rise out towards the lilies. Fortuitously perhaps, my cast missed the centre of the dying rings by some distance. Before I had time to re-cast, the fish rose again, this time a little nearer to the defiantly bobbing artificial. Agonisingly slowly, my quarry moved nearer, dimpling the surface gently at regular intervals to mark his progress. Gradually, my world shrank smaller until my entire consciousness was contained within a foot's radius of the end of the cast. Despite the fading light, I seemed to see the tiny fly with heightened clarity. It had sunk a little now to slouch lower in the surface film – a good sign, I knew from experience.

As the fish continued its unhurried progress, time stood still. So imperceptible was the change in the water's surface when it came, that I almost failed to notice. The only difference was that the fly was no longer there, sucked noiselessly beneath the surface.

Instinctively, I raised the tip of the rod. In an instant, reality was restored and the peaceful tableau was broken. I straightened from my crouch, almost slipping from the bank in my excitement. In a flurry of glistening droplets, the fish thrashed the surface wildly, then dashed determinedly towards the lily pads. I knew from bitter experience that once there he would be as good as lost: two-pound nylon would not stand a chance. And this was no half-pounder: this was something altogether bigger.

Awakening to the danger just in time, I applied enough pressure to divert my quarry from his goal. Another protracted bout of tail thrashing followed, turning the still surface to a furious foam. I looked on helplessly with my heart in my mouth. Then abruptly, he dove deep and for several minutes the battle became a dour struggle, pitting angler against unseen adversary.

At last, he began to weaken. For the first time, I had the rod tip high. Gently, I began to guide him towards the net. Not done yet, he made one last, despairing bid for freedom, slapping the surface again with a broad, wedge-like tail and revealing for the first time, a golden flank spotted red and black.

But this time I could feel his strength waning. Another moment and I was drawing the heaving flank of my quarry carefully over the rim of the net, heedless now of the chill water lapping around the top of my walking boots and seeping slowly into my socks.

Out over the sea, the sun was no more than a memory, its afterglow fading to a pale orange along the horizon. I turned for one last look towards the edge of the world. The sea disappeared from view as we dropped down towards the glen and the haven of Kinloch Bay.

Tired and content, the city and its pressures seemed a long way off. Unbidden, memories returned of a small boy in a city church, only half listening to the words of the silver-haired preacher from the islands. His theme had confused the young mind. Heaven was on earth, he had said, if only we looked for it.

Over all these years, the message had lain there, dormant, biding its time. Now, at last, I understood.

Above: Approaching Rum aboard the *Loch Arkaig*
Below: Once the preserve of the rich: Rum's Kinloch Castle

PART IV
EXPANDING HORIZONS

Freed from the shackles of family, home and the rules that go with them, many drift away from childhood pastimes. But for me, as yet unconcerned by the growing unemployment and despair all around, fishing became almost more important, an antidote to the frenetic late nights, laughter and limited perspective of student existence, even at the heart of a hard-bitten city like Glasgow. In its way, fishing became an opportunity to escape, to reflect on the painful experiences of growing up and to think them through with friends from a comfortably similar background.

By far the most painful experience was Jenny, whom I discovered in a dingy second-class compartment on an overnight train from Glasgow to London, en route for Paris. Jenny, with the beautifully rich and expressive accent, the impossibly deep brown eyes and the totally offbeat sense of humour. Jenny, who drank pints, chain-smoked and wore outrageous earrings and daringly short skirts. Jenny, who vanished from my life only to re-appear two years later on my parents' doorstep with a toddler in tow, ruffling momentarily the calm of Morningside on a Sunday morning.

1

FIRST IMPRESSIONS

The education system is definitely not what it used to be. When I was a student, the Education Authority grant covered the essentials (beer, food, rent, sport and parties) with just about enough left over for the thrifty amongst us to buy the odd textbook. These days, however, it must be difficult for the average student to pay the rent, never mind actually enjoy the precious privileges of student life.

In retrospect, I consider myself to have been one of the 'lucky' ones; we accepted that in a jobless Scotland things would get no better. We knew that on a student grant, with a student's aspirations, we were first amongst the rich. We could afford our round when it came along and that was all that mattered. The future's bleak prospects of unemployment could take care of themselves.

I soon discovered that if I lived at home in the holidays, shamelessly exploiting parental generosity, I could even put away enough to manage a few days' trout fishing. So each year, when the holidays finally arrived, it was to the remote lochs of Forsinard amidst the rolling peat flows of Sutherland that I headed. Inaccessible except to the young and fit or to those with the money and excuses to warrant a ghillie and an argocat ride, Sletill, Leir, Talaheel and the rest lay five, six, even seven miles out over rough moors, crisp and springy in dry weather, soft and clinging in wet. We would curse and swear on the way out, legs aching, brows sweating, tackle heavy on our backs, at one and the same time regretting a winter of student excesses and wondering what could be worth this torture.

But when we finally reached our destination, tiredness sloughed from us like a second skin, leaving only eagerness, excitement and appreciation of the sheer wildness of the place. And make no mistake about it, the Forsinard lochs offered some of the finest wild brown trout fishing anywhere in the world.

Loch Sletill, in particular, provided magnificent sport, its two types of trout as different as if they were separate species. The silvery trout, generally weighing in the half to three-quarter pound range, were omnipresent and fought with carefree abandon, throwing themselves into the air like sea-fresh finnock.

If such were the hors d'oeuvre, then the 'golden-bellies', heavy fish weighing from one to two pounds or more, provided the main course. These glorious specimens rarely took the surface fly unless the wind was up and the waves were high and crested with foam. Then the fishing took on a new dimension. In the peak of condition from a rich diet of shrimp and snail on Sletill's stony bottom, the golden-bellies took with confidence and fought with all the snarling strength of tigers.

In two years fishing at Forsinard, our best bags from Sletill were nine fish at eight pounds and twenty at sixteen pounds, both to just two rods and in only a few hours' fishing. Some years later, with the lochs now accessible by car and the moors blanket-planted with conifers, I returned with my wife. Our best bag, from several outings, was eight fish for just over four pounds.

But it was on the tiny Clach, not Sletill, that we encountered the biggest trout. Clach was the most accessible of the Forsinard lochs, little more than an overgrown peat hag sitting on the plateau overlooking Strath Halladale. Unlike the other lochs, its waters were dark and peat-stained, and its vertical banks disappeared abruptly beneath the angler's feet. During our first visit we had spent the better part of a day on Clach until frustration had driven us to walk on over the moors to Talaheel to save a blank day. We had not seen a fish and could barely imagine one inhabiting these forbidding waters.

In the bar that night, Richard McNicol, ghillie on the hotel's waters, assured us that there were trout in Clach, and big trout at that. Not convinced, we did not hurry back. After all, with the wealth of good fishing available to us, why risk another fruitless and frustrating day? And anyway, Richard had had a few drinks …

It was our second summer at Forsinard. The weather was more suited to sunbathing than fishing, the sun a ball of fire blazing from an azure blue sky with not a cloud for days.

We had fished hard, stalking the occasional rise with stealth, aiming to

Promising conditions on Loch Sletill, Caithness

place the fly promptly in the middle of the fading rings. Success in such conditions was gratifying and we had returned from Sletill that day buoyant, weighed down by a beautiful bag of twelve silvery trout.

Suitably changed and refreshed with a good meal, it was the usual practice to pass the evening nursing a beer and talking of plans for the morrow. But tonight the air was so warm and inviting that we were tempted to try our luck again. We had often pondered on the potential of dusk fishing, but contentment and the soporific effects of a good dinner, allied to the sure knowledge that only dour little Clach was accessible enough for such a venture, usually put paid to any action.

That night, however, with conditions perfect and the seed already sown in our minds, we needed to go just to lay the ghost of our curiosity. So, armed with a heavy dose of scepticism, we set off for Clach. A short drive and a sharp climb from the end of the little dirt track and we were there. The evening air was fresh and clear, and carried on it the guttural calls of grouse settling for the night. Dark Clach was like a mirror, reflecting the purples and greens of heather on the distant slopes of Sletill Hill. But apart from a delicate ripple which spread out over the centre of the loch, fading like a ghost into the margins, everything was still.

And so it remained, not greatly to our surprise, until the last light had almost gone and only a faint afterglow remained to illuminate the distant horizon. The occasional moth fluttered from amongst the heather and danced defiantly out over the loch. From time to time, a sedge would skitter randomly across the still surface for all the world like a tiny motor boat bereft of helmsman. We were on the verge of calling it a day and heading back in time for last call at the bar. There was the prospect of a long walk over to Leir in the morning and, anyway, we had not expected in our heart of hearts to catch anything from this uncompromising little loch.

And that was when I felt that subtle change in the atmosphere, impossible to describe, but unmistakable to the experienced fisher. Immediately, all my senses jolted into alertness. From the boat, my companion was already pointing agitatedly towards a series of concentric ripples which spread gently out by the weed bed.

'So there are fish in Clach,' I mused. As if in confirmation, a snout broke the surface lazily, halfway between me and the boat. It seemed like an eternity before the dorsal fin appeared, waving like the sail on an olden-day clipper. As I watched, a broad wedge-shaped tail followed. So leisurely was the rise that it seemed as though I watched in slow motion an action replay of some event long past.

While I remained frozen in immobility, that seemingly lifeless stretch of water came alive with rising trout, as if some invisible signal had declared the evening rise open. I swore quietly under my breath, almost unable to take in the evidence before my eyes. These were the confident, unhurried rises of big trout, heading and tailing like fish that knew their business and were not about to be side-tracked.

Before I could recover my poise, there was another shout from the direction of the boat. My friend's rod was bent almost double and a sizeable bow wave made steady progress towards the far bank accompanied by the agitated scream of reel. I looked on for a while in excitement, perhaps tinged with just the merest hint of envy.

Then, out the corner of my eye, I spotted two fish rising almost simultaneously at the very edge of my own casting range. They looked enormous from where I stood, perhaps five pounds or maybe even more.

Full of anticipation, imagining already the powerful surge of the taking fish, I cast towards the nearest rise. But try as I might, I could not generate even the slightest interest. The fish continued to rise for a time, seemingly unperturbed by my increasingly frenzied attentions, then cruised unhurriedly off leaving only a bulge in the surface film and an ache in my heart to mark its stately progress.

By now, my friend's battle was nearing its conclusion. Reeling in and peering intently into the gloom, I could just make out foam where the fish thrashed desperately on the surface. Then I heard the unmistakable cry of triumph and saw the water broken as net and fish were heaved to safety.

That fish tipped the scales at just an ounce short of three pounds; my companion was convinced it was the smallest fish he had seen rise. We returned home jubilant, already planning tactics for the following evening.

That night the weather changed and storms set in for the rest of our stay.

But the story does not quite end there.

Some years later, in my professional capacity, I had cause to peruse the results of a government research survey of the fish population over a wide area of north Scotland. A familiar name and Ordnance Survey map reference caught my eye. 'Clach', the entry read, 'fishless ...'

2

A COSTLY BUSINESS

In these days of high-tech equipment, fishing can be an expensive pastime. This is particularly true for those of us who are habitually accident-prone and it is the principal reason why, for many years now, I have done almost all my fishing with the same rod.

To anyone schooled on the luxuries of carbon-fibre, I am sure my trusty fibreglass 'Little Lake' must appear an unwieldy club. But to a youngster with wrists strengthened from years of toil with a Greenheart monster from pre-war days, it seemed impossibly light and a joy to cast. Now, all these years on, it is like an old friend in whose company I am totally at ease. Somehow, I cannot imagine feeling remotely as comfortable with several hundred pounds worth of finely tuned carbon-fibre in my clumsy hands. Yet,

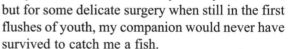

but for some delicate surgery when still in the first flushes of youth, my companion would never have survived to catch me a fish.

That first outing with my prized new possession was to a favourite little loch high in the hills above Loch Rannoch. To reach Finnart involved a bumpy drive and a sharp climb through some of the most majestic remnants of the old Caledonian pine forest, through stands of trees with massive boles pitted from centuries of bleak Highland winters, trees with memories extending back to the Jacobite uprisings and beyond. On through dappled shade and sunlight, across magical moss-carpeted glades, through knee-deep heather and thickets of bracken, tight fronds thrusting boldly towards the spring sunshine.

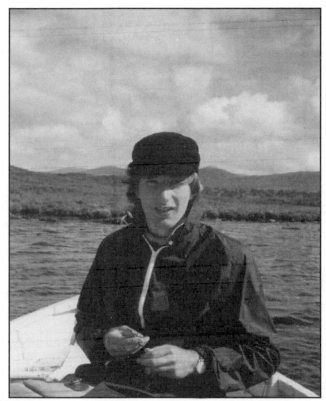

Above: **A cold breeze on Finnart, Perthshire**
Below: **The Mentieth rainbow (top) that cost me a line**

The loch itself is a patchwork of tree-clad islands and sheltered bays, windswept headlands and rocky outcrops interspersed with quiet reed-fringed bays. Interesting to explore and exciting to fish, always tensely anticipating the explosive rise of a wild brownie hurtling from the peat-stained depths, the angler is left with a pounding heart and, more often than not, cursing sluggish reactions.

On the day in question, I was sharing a boat with my father, a state of affairs that led me over the years to take certain precautions regardless of the prevailing meteorological conditions. A hat, sunglasses and a turned-up collar became characteristic uniform in just the way that England's opening batsmen would not consider facing the West Indies on the hallowed turf of Lords or in the heady atmosphere of Sabina Park without thigh pads, arm guards, helmet and sundry other protective accoutrements.

On this occasion at least, the expectation and high spirits with which I invariably set forth seemed justified. Within seconds, a healthy rise shattered the quiet surface off to the right of the gently drifting boat. My father sprang into action. With the benefit of experience, however, I swayed out of the way with an easy nonchalance which would have sent the phlegmatic Geoffrey Boycott into raptures. As anticipated, the boat rocked violently and a team of wet flies swished through the air where moments before my head had been.

Perhaps complacency, however, was my undoing. For next moment, my treasured new rod kicked in my hand like a live thing and I could only look on in horror as half of the glinting new top section flew in a graceful arc towards the dying rings of the rising trout, my father's size ten Bloody Butcher firmly embedded.

For the record, I fished on that day with my old rod but caught nothing of note; somehow the gloss had gone from the day.

That was by no means my only unexpectedly expensive day's fishing.

Some years later, I found myself fishing with a friend on the Lake of Menteith in Perthshire. A different proposition altogether to Finnart, Menteith is a big water set in farming land against the pretty backdrop of the Trossachs. As befits a water which claims the distinction of being Scotland's only lake, it is positively steeped in history. Each summer, visitors make the short trip to the tree-clad island of Inchmahome to visit the ruins of the Augustinian monastery where, it is rumoured, the redoubtable Mary Queen of Scots was once incarcerated.

Much more important to the keen fisher, Menteith is one of Scotland's foremost trout fisheries. I particularly enjoyed our trips to The Lake; we had got to know Billy, the fishery manager, and always had a lively chat before we set out. One of life's enthusiasts, Billy invariably raised our expectations and sent us forth full of hope. Leaning idly against the rails of a trout cage, rolling a cigarette between practised fingers, he would regale us with tales of huge trout until our anticipation got the better of us and we could wait no longer.

Today, a strong north-west wind was whipping up a daunting wave. We had fished all morning in the relative shelter of the Big Bay, out of the worst of the wind's effects. But with Billy's tales of record catches from the Heronry ringing in our ears, it was not long before discretion lost out and the temptation to risk crossing to the south side of the lake became irresistible. It was an exhilarating experience, the sturdy, clinker-built boat slamming into wave after wave, spray drenching us as my friend held the boat on course with a mixture of skill and brute force.

That day, the Heronry caught the full force of the wind and even with the drogue biting deep we found ourselves drifting almost faster than we could retrieve our casts. The wisdom of our decision began to look dubious as the shore loomed up ahead, the noise deafening as the waves lashed the shallows into a foaming maelstrom. I glanced towards my companion, catching his eye and agreeing wordlessly: one more cast was all we could afford. If we got caught in the shallows we might never get out.

With an obdurate perversity, my rod tip chose that precise moment to arch over as the point fly was engulfed in an explosion of froth and frenzied trout. Impossibly far away, it seemed, a large rainbow trout danced across the wave tops in a spirited show of defiance. It took a warning shout from the other end of the boat to remind me of our peril. Urged on by my companion, I applied dangerously heavy-handed tactics, netting a gallant opponent at the first attempt as he still kicked wildly. This was no limp 'stockie'; this was an over-wintered fish, perfect in every spot and fin, the essence of rainbow trout, wild and strong as his free-running steelhead cousins.

The engine kicked into life and the boat jumped forward, wrenching me from my state of awed reverie. In the same moment, my rod tip bucked and my reel screamed for the second time in as many minutes. I looked up in bewilderment. This time, there was no silvery missile cutting through the waves in a bid for freedom. The terrible truth dawned on me; my line was already down to the backing, the business end hissing audibly as it disappeared over the side of the boat into the water churning around the outboard propeller. Galvanised belatedly into action, I lunged past my companion to cut the motor. Too late. The engine coughed, spluttered and fell silent before I could reach it.

When the sad remnants of my double-tapered floating line were finally cut from the propeller blades and the boat was once more sea-worthy, we were wet through, bad-tempered and thoroughly aground.

More recently still, I had a salutory and costly experience on quite a different water. I was fishing the Wharfe, a remarkably productive and well-managed trout stream that wends its way across the moors of North Yorkshire, dropping through the occasional spectacular gorge, full of rushing water and hefty waterfalls, on its way to join the Ouse just north of Selby. I had got wet before, shipped water over the top of my waders many times and sunk into bogs over my walking boots on occasions too numerous to count. But, believe it or not, I had never actually fallen in.

So when the inevitable happened, it not only came as a complete surprise but also left me to make a somewhat uncomfortable analysis of the dangers of fishing alone.

The day had started warm, with a gentle breeze, the occasional burst of sunlight playing on the water through the heavy boughs of overhanging beech in full summer garb. But it had not taken long for a brooding cloud cover to roll in and hide the sun for good. The wind had strengthened and veered around to blow directly upriver, rendering downstream nymphing awkward, if not impossible. I had already donned a jersey and a heavy coat. I was thinking more about the flask of coffee in the car and the teatime cricket scores, than the fishing.

To be honest, I do not know exactly how it happened. One minute I was wading across the current in an effort to get a bit closer to that awkward but inviting run under the far bank, the next I was completely immersed in unseasonally cold water, waders filling rapidly and threatening to upend me at any moment. I had, for just a brief instant, a trout's eye view of the streambed. Stoneflies scuttled for cover amongst the moss like a host of tiny dinosaurs disturbed from their routine by my ungainly intrusion. Streamers of crowsfoot waved in the current, medieval pennants fluttering cheerfully on the breeze.

Perla cortubianm
Stonefly

On reflection, my accident was probably the result of a combination of things: inattention, slick stones, old waders with little or no grip and a sense of balance that was not what it had been 20 years before. Either way, I somehow managed to right myself, flounder gracelessly to the bank and flop onto the cropped grass of the rabbit warren. I sat there shivering for a few minutes before my composure returned sufficiently to empty waders and check tackle. In dismay, I realised that the tip section of my rod was badly bent and that my favourite trout bass was disappearing rapidly downstream towards the next pool, never to be seen again.

It was round about then that I vowed, not for the first (or last) time, to trade in my rod and tackle for a set of golf clubs at the first opportunity.

Fortunately, however, promises are made to be broken. Mellowing over a whisky some hours later, I decided that checked slacks and v-necked sweaters were just not my style.

3

ONE TO WRITE HOME ABOUT

A true pessimist, of course, would not see it this way, but pessimism does have one major advantage. Just occasionally, life has a pleasant surprise in store.

Like the day I caught what was, at the time, my best river trout. I was fishing the Dochart in Perthshire, a river which is not renowned for big trout. Since my early days worming on Highland burns and Border streams, most of my fishing had been on the hill lochs. While I was then and still remain, totally bewitched by the magical, living qualities of moving water, my river fishing experience could best be described as extremely limited.

So I set out with no great expectations. I certainly did not put the local taxidermist on standby. In fact, I did not even bother to pack a bag for the catch.

As it turned out, it was one of those rare, late spring days that, remembered years later, needs no rose-tinted glasses to enhance its perfection. On such a day, I could not help but concur with Roderick Haig-Brown's observation that 'a river is water in its loveliest form.' A gentle sun sparkled off the merry surface as happy, gurgling stickles gave way to swirling pools. Pools that might, to one of a more naturally optimistic bent, have seemed rich with the promise of trout.

From the tangle of birch and bramble along the bank, a resonant chorus of birdsong heralded the summer to come. A cuckoo provided an occasional, joyous counterpoint. I relaxed totally into my surroundings, yet my pessimism, if anything, grew perversely stronger. If I had ever nurtured even the tiniest seed of hope, it failed completely to germinate. Catching a fish on such a day was asking altogether too much.

I had fished this pool once already that morning. The perfect run at its head gave way gradually to a foam-flecked stillness and finally, to the smooth glide which slid away over a gravel bed and into a short stretch of broken water punctuated by moss-covered rocks, a favourite resting place for a patrolling dipper. The water was not deep and I was able to wade half way across to fish from directly upstream, letting my flies drift down the streaming water and hang for a brief moment, tantalisingly I hoped, where the current began to ease.

What happened on my first cast was both so unexpected and so close to perfection as to be the stuff of sheer fantasy. The flies swung round into the stream, Kingfisher Butcher on the point. I imagined them hanging for the merest blink of an eye in that tiny void, caught momentarily between natural movement and unnatural drag. In that moment, I sensed, rather than felt, the firm take of a confident trout.

For a second, I assumed it had to be small. But the sudden flurry of strenuous activity in the streaming water below quickly dispelled the thought and I stumbled in shock, close to shipping water over my wader tops. The fish bolted for a deep hole amongst tangled willow roots under the far bank. A family of frightened mallard squawked loudly and took to the air in a rush of feathers and water.

Twice the fish ran the length of the pool, taking line from the reel; twice I let him go, then gradually recovered the line, all the time edging carefully from the fast water towards the gravel spit where I had left my landing net. I could only pray that he would not be inspired to make for the broken water below the pool. If he did, I would surely lose him: there was no way of following.

But today, against the odds, luck was on my side. Finally, I saw my quarry, energy clearly waning, on the surface. I drew in a sharp breath, awed by his length and the depth of his heaving golden sides. In seconds, it was over. The fish lay in the lush grass and I sat quietly, as ever, watching as the sparkling flanks dulled, toasting a worthy opponent in my mind, listening as my heartbeat returned to normal. All the while, still, hardly daring to believe.

End of a perfect day

PART V

IN THE DOLDRUMS

For a period during the eighties I became a statistic, just another of the unemployed masses. This, despite seven years at University studying environmental science, a discipline billed by over-zealous career guidance councillors as the subject of the future. For me, as for many of my contemporaries, the future was proving elusive.

Back home in placid Morningside, a world away from Glasgow and the stark, brooding silence of the Clydeside shipyards where the massive cranes pointed skywards in supplication and gathered rust, my parents had moved to a smaller flatted property, no doubt welcoming the peace and quiet which should, by rights, follow when the family had finally left the nest.

My sister and I returned home just months apart. My parents responded, or so it seemed, by installing a burglar alarm: one of those unsmiling devices which permits just thirty seconds to unlock the front door and key-in the correct number. I well remember standing on the doorstep in the bitter cold of early morning Edinburgh, willing myself sober enough to pass the test.

During daylight hours I became a full-time author of job applications. The letters of rejection piled higher; life was on hold.

DAVID'S BOAT COMES IN!

Records are made to be broken. Such might be the accepted wisdom but in thirty years fishing, I have never broken a record of any sort, leastways not an official one. My best (indeed only) salmon weighed ten pounds, my biggest sea trout just two pounds, one ounce, and I have yet to catch a three pound trout, despite many close shaves.

For all that, I have had a couple of brief moments in the fishing limelight, albeit the first was without the fanfare, the photographers and the media interviews.

The day began no differently to any other Saturday fishing trip. We set out early to avoid the traffic and to make the most of the day. Passing through Perth as the city was just beginning to shake itself into wakefulness, we stopped briefly at our favourite baker's shop to top up picnic boxes with pies and buns still fresh from the oven. It was a time-honoured part of the tradition which I always enjoyed. The exquisite aroma of fresh bread mixed with the spicy tang of sweetmeats excited and stimulated senses only slowly awakening from slumber. By the time we left the city behind, we were alert, the anticipation was mounting, and we really felt we were on our way.

Collecting the boat keys from the caravan park was the next part of the ritual. By the time we reached Pitlochry this particular morning, the weather had turned cold and dark clouds were massing threateningly on the horizon. If only to raise our hopes, we desperately needed our customary chat with the gatekeeper.

As usual, Mr Clark was waiting for us, arms resting on the top bar of the gate, ruddy face glowing with the cold. His worn tweed jacket was as crumpled as ever and the battered old deerstalker sat on his head as if surgically attached to his scalp. We had learned from experience that a few minutes talking to Mr Clark was time well-spent. Not only did his enthusiasm work wonders for our confidence when prospects looked bleak but we invariably left furnished with much valuable information about the lochs and how they were fishing.

Today, almost before we got out of the car, we could sense barely disguised excitement beneath the unruffled exterior; clearly, something out of the ordinary was afoot. For a while, our friend strove heroically to maintain an appropriate air of decorum and the conversation flitted over the usual mundane topics: the weather; recent catches; the tourist trade in Pitlochry. Then, at last, the dam broke and out it all poured in an undignified rush. The Fisheries Laboratory had been developing food supplements for farm-reared American brook trout and, at the end of their experiments, had gifted to the angling club a batch of top-quality fish. These had been stocked in Loch Bhac, our destination, and Mr Clark was confident that the loch would soon produce a fish to top the existing British rod-caught record for the species, which at that time (before brookies had become an accepted part of the fly-fishing scene), stood at a modest two pounds, seven ounces. Today could be the day.

Inspired by this news, the unfriendly weather was temporarily forgotten and we could not get to the loch quick enough. Up the track through the forestry plantation, taking corners like refugees from the RAC rally, skidding finally to a stop in the rough little car park deep in the forest. We tackled up in record time and soon strode purposefully through the trees along the line of the drainage ditch until Bhac came into view.

And that was when our enthusiasm sustained its first real blow. Emerging from the shelter of the trees, the biting north wind hit us square in the face but even that did not prepare me for the sight which greeted my smarting eyes; all along the exposed bank, the loch was rimmed with a crust of snow. In other circumstances, the beauty of the scene might have enraptured but not today. This was spring for goodness sake; this was the fishing season. Where were the hatching mayfly and the gentle rings of rising trout eager to sate their hunger after a long, hard winter?

Somewhat deflated, we bailed the boat in silence, pushed it from the bank and started drifting. By mid-afternoon, our numbers were depleted. My father had returned to the car to listen to the Grand National on the radio. The conditions at Aintree were 'good to firm' and, according to Peter O'Sullivan, the spectators were basking in the spring sunshine in shirtsleeves. What a difference a few hundred miles can make.

My friend and I liked to think we were made of sterner stuff and we persevered a little longer. By now, dreams of doing battle with record-breaking brook trout had given way to the simple desire to catch a fish, any fish, just to stir the blood and stimulate the circulation. But it seemed it was not to be.

Patience stretched to the limit, we decided to take an oar each and row once round the loch, sinking lines trailing behind, as much to bring life to frozen limbs as with any real expectation of breaking our collective duck. It was a hard pull into the strengthening wind and we made slow progress across the most exposed and deepest part of the loch, so slow that our flies had ample opportunity to sink and to fish well down in the water.

It was about then that my rod suddenly bucked and line started to screech from the reel. Numbed perhaps, by the cold, it took me a moment to realise what was happening. When the penny finally dropped, I lurched clumsily into action, dropping the oar to make a grab for the rod and nearly capsizing the boat in the process. The battle was a dour one, the fish was deep and some distance from the boat, so it was not until the final moments that I caught my first glimpse: a dark shape spiralling into view like some great shark emerging from the depths. There could be little doubt; it was a brook trout and a big one at that.

Moments later, my companion carefully slipped the net under his flank and hauled him into the boat: two pounds, ten ounces of fishy perfection, deep of belly, full fins edged with the striking white trim characteristic of the species. For a while I looked on in awe, the moment spoilt only by the niggling disappointment that it had taken such underhand measures to catch him. For the purpose of interviews and articles in the angling press, I decided pompously, the official version would be: 'Black Pennell, fished deep …' My secret would be safe.

When at last we returned to the car, soaked now by the driving rain bearing down relentlessly from the north, my father emerged from behind steamed windows with a triumphant expression on his face. I let him play his card first: Red Rum had confounded his detractors and won the National again. Then I produced my ace …

But fame, they say, is an illusion. And for me that day, it proved to be so. When we returned, elated, to the gatehouse, armed with boat keys and bearing trophy aloft, only disappointment awaited us. A three pound, two ounce fish had been taken that same afternoon from one of the other lochs. Perhaps, given my guilty secret, it was all I deserved.

My second brush with fame came two years later almost to the day. This time I was fishing the Lake of Menteith and again it was my first outing of the season. As on Bhac, the weather was doing its spiteful best to impersonate the depths of winter.

The fish, when it came, was nothing out of the ordinary: a small rainbow, no more than twelve or thirteen ounces. So ordinary, in fact, that it was almost consigned to the fish bass before I noticed the tag attached firmly behind the dorsal fin. When I did spot it, I realised right away that this was not a normal fishery tag; it did, in fact, belong to a certain popular Sunday newspaper which had recently launched a competition on a number of Scottish fisheries to boost publicity.

I had surreptitiously perused the pages of the said paper from time to time, out of curiosity only of course, and I was aware that tagged fish commanded a healthy prize. Furthermore, the more noteworthy catches were reported in the paper each weekend.

The question was how to turn a three-quarter pound rainbow caught on a Missionary into something worthy of newspaper coverage. It was not my first ever trout, I had not caught it while eating lunch with my cast idly trailing behind the boat, I was not even using a fly given to me by a little green man from an alien spacecraft.

The answer came to me in the car on the way home; it was easy really. All I had to do when I phoned the paper was to tell them that I was a student studying for a degree in Fisheries Management. Actually, I was studying for a degree in Ecology and taking Fisheries Management as one of my honours options but that, I felt, was somewhat superfluous detail.

And, sure enough, it worked! The headline the following Sunday read: 'David's Boat Comes In.' Beneath, the text stated that I was in my 'final year studying for an honours degree in (would you believe?), Fisheries Management!'

So, I mused smugly over Sunday breakfast. A valuable lesson had been learnt about media manipulation. It's all in a day's fishing!

2

IN THE LAP OF THE GODS

A las, I am not one of these fishing writers for whom time and money seem to be no object. I am a mere mortal, whose angling must be fitted around work, family and other constraints. Neither does my job bring me into contact with those who boast the rights to fishing on expensive salmon beats (or anywhere else for that matter). Perhaps I should have been a lawyer or a bank manager.

For us ordinary folk, money spent on fishing permits must be balanced against the weekly shopping bill, the price of petrol and the monthly mortgage payments. That is why I look forward so much to my fishing holiday: five or six days annually when fishing becomes the prime consideration.

Relying on pre-determined dates, however, is hazardous, if also unavoidable. Leave must be booked months in advance, school holidays must be considered. I have lost count of the number of times I have arrived at my destination to be greeted with the words: 'You should have been here last week.' Or worse still, the occasions I have left with enthusiastic protestations that 'next week should be perfect' ringing in my ears.

Take my very first fishing holiday, a week's spring fishing for trout on the Aberdeenshire Don, a fine trout river with a reputation for producing wild fish of a size and quality unparalleled by other Scottish rivers. Even now, the prospect conjures images of bluebell-carpeted woods, warming sunshine and bursting leaves, air alive with the sound of splashing trout and screaming reels.

We drove north from Edinburgh in a ferment of excitement, my father and I, weighed down with advice and new tackle bought especially for the occasion. Even before we unpacked, we took a stroll down to the stone bridge and leaned on the lichen-encrusted parapet to watch hungry fish rising to a prolific hatch of spring mayfly, just how it was meant to be. Fluttering from the margins in droves, the flies were intercepted with such carefree abandon that our success on the morrow seemed assured.

All around us, spring was in full bloom, the very air carried the scent of summer to come. We went to bed content and filled with anticipation.

The following morning, I was first to rise and first to open the curtains. The scene that met my bleary gaze made me pinch myself to see if I was still dreaming. In the car park below, my father's bright yellow Renault was invisible, not a common occurrence in itself, but the reason was still more unlikely. The car was buried deep beneath a blanket of dazzlingly fresh snow.

For six days we struggled to keep our hands from numbness and our rod rings from freezing. The sparkling beauty of the landscape which might, in another situation, have held us spellbound, was lost on us. Each evening, we sat thawing out over cock-a-leekie soup, venison or locally produced beef, assuring one another that it could not possibly last.

And, of course, we were right. When we arose on the morning of our departure, the snow had vanished, the sun shone warmly on a benign landscape and, once more, gentle rises dimpled the surface of the bridge pool. It was as if the intervening period had not happened.

And then there was that first trip to Forsinard. Granted, the main object of our attention was the trout fishing in the hill lochs but secretly, both my friend and I had more than half an eye for the Halladale and her salmon.

We arrived during an extended period of drought almost unprecedented in the area. The little Halladale threaded her way down the Strath like the backbone of a dry and dusty skeleton; the salmon stranded in her shrunken, rocky pools were darkly coloured and splashed in sullen discontentment from time to time. There was not even the remotest chance of hooking one in the oily, sluggish depths to which they had retreated.

That is how it remained until our last day; then the sky darkened, the heavens opened and rain drove in sheets across the moors to batter loudly against the windows of the hotel and bring fresh fish streaming up the Halladale in urgent waves of silver. As we drove home across the watershed, dropping down towards the little fishing village of Helmsdale along the banks of the Helmsdale River, we could not fail to notice anglers striding purposefully, fingers hooked through the gills of sea-fresh salmon, or others with rods bent mightily by heavy fish which had come up on the overnight spate.

All we could do was curse and think of next year.

And then there was that trip to Scourie on the far north-west coast. We did see and catch the odd fish, a tribute as much to the quality of the fishing as to our perseverance, but it was hard work as temperatures soared daily towards thirty degrees centigrade and the clear skies remained completely unsullied by cloud of any description.

A more recent fishing holiday, spent on the west coast of Ireland with my wife, barely even accorded us the consolation of a fish or two. The scenery was wonderful, the people open and friendly and the Guinness fit for a king but we still spent four frustrating days on Lough Corrib before we saw evidence that the famous mayfly lough did, in fact, contain a fish. And even then, all we saw was a distant splash which might well have been a mirage, the product of desperate minds. Our total catch for the week, if you discount a few game little fish taken during a couple of hours' light relief on the hill lochs, was a resounding zero.

But perhaps, in highlighting these failures, I am putting an unfair slant on the merits of the fishing holiday. I have had successful holidays and even when the fishing has not lived up to expectations, I have found enjoyment in other, more important, ways.

The proof of the pudding is in the eating. I continue to return whenever I can, undaunted by failure. When fishing is limited by considerations of time and money, those precious days of escape become more valuable than ever; all you can do is accept the risk that comes with the territory and meet whatever the gods throw at you with equanimity.

Difficult conditions on Lough Corrib, Eire

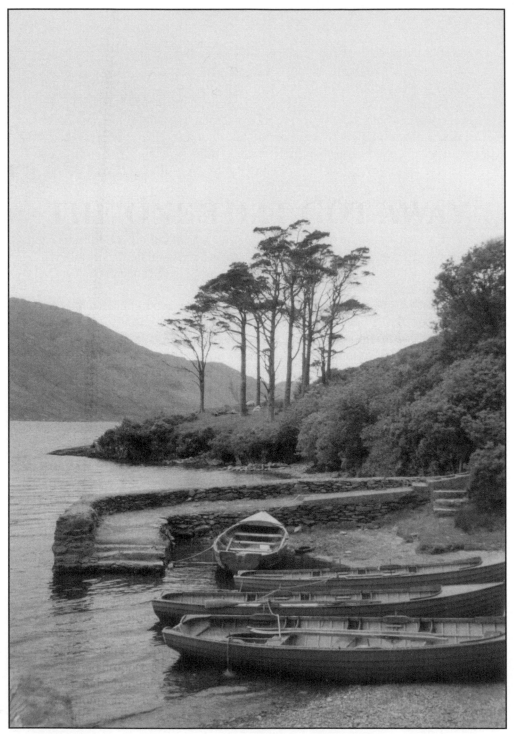

Clouding over nicely but it's time to leave for home. Lough Corrib, Eire, 1995

PART VI
LAYING FOUNDATIONS

Inevitably, the job when it came, was located in the relative affluence of the Home Counties amidst the rolling countryside and gentle climate of the Chilterns. I drove south with a mixture of elation and optimism, nervousness and excitement, sitting proudly at the wheel of my first car, a bright orange Opel Kadet, purchased with a hefty loan.

The day fitted the occasion. I left behind a dour Scotland, driving across the border amidst angry snow flurries, black storm clouds crowding the view in the wing mirror, to arrive in the little village of Skirmett to the welcoming fanfare of a spring cuckoo bearing her soul in the gentle shirt-sleeve sunshine.

I had my first pint of Brakspear's that week in the tight confines of the little 'Ship' bar in nearby Marlow. As I ordered a 'bitter', remembering just in time to resist the urge to ask for a pint of 'heavy', my falseness was quickly rumbled. The middle-aged man sitting on the barstool deeply engrossed in his pint, jerked his head in my direction and informed me in an incongruously heavy Glasgow brogue that I 'wasnae frae here'.

He had a family, this man, and no job. Taking the politicians' pompous words to heart, he had got on his bike (a battered old scooter) and he had travelled south, like me, to seek work. Why to Marlow? Because that's where the pin had stuck in the map.

1

STRANGER
IN A STRANGE LAND

L ooking back, I was not really the angry young man I might have been. Yes, frustrated after two years with no income and an uncertain future. Yes, nervous about what lay ahead. And yes, sad to be leaving the lochs and burns of home so far behind. But, at the time, all this was swamped by an overwhelming sense of relief, relief at finding a job, relief at rediscovering my sense of worth, relief at pressing 'go' once again.

It was not until the end of my first week that I began to realise I had entered a different world, a world where I was the exception rather than the rule. I was having a quiet drink in the incongruously named Argyll Pub in Henley-on-Thames, resplendent in its tartan décor, walls adorned with dusty prints of sombre Highland chieftains. When I paid, unthinking, using the last remnants of the cash I had brought with me, the barman held my Scottish pound note up to the light, scrutinised Robert the Bruce closely, looked sideways at me and declined to accept any further business. My fourteenth century countryman would undoubtedly have exited with the man's head impaled on his claymore. Discretion, however, pulled rank and I left with rather less fuss, feeling suddenly very foreign.

I soon learned that the English attitude to fishing and to most other things that mattered to me, was indisputably different. This might seem strange, given that Scotland and England are not only neighbours but close neighbours separated by a boundary arbitrary enough to permit Berwick Rangers to play in the Scottish football league and Mike Denness to captain the England cricket team. For me, certainly, this one, incontrovertible fact took a whole lot of getting used to.

Such extreme cultural emancipation may owe something to the

profound distrust with which the Scots have always viewed the English, even though most Scots these days actually do not have to look too closely at the family tree to trace an element of English lineage in themselves. It may even reflect the genuine historical peculiarities that mark the Scots as a downtrodden race constantly resisting subjugation by the cruel bully on its border. More likely, however, it is a consequence of the stark environmental, climatic and (frequently) economic differences that cannot help but assault the senses of the discerning traveller: differences which any nation other than Scotland might be expected to minimise, if not actively suppress, at every possible opportunity.

With characteristic perversity, we Scots, however, are morbidly proud of the harshness of life in the northern extremities of the British Isles. It gives us endless potential to indulge two of our favourite pastimes: introversion and melancholy. From the works of Stevenson and Scott right through to Ian Rankin's modern day crime writings, no Scottish drama is complete unless played out against a bleak backdrop of cold, grey, puritanical drizzle and stark urban decay.

Of course, everything is a matter of degree. The closest the average city-dwelling Scot gets to a 'wilderness experience' is in reality, ten minutes between showers huddled around a collapsible picnic table in a lay-by somewhere between Fort Augustus and Drumnadrochit on the annual family holiday. Yet there is not a Scot alive who does not see himself privately as something of a claymore-weilding, kilted rebel striding through a wild, rugged landscape of tumbling burns, shaggy cartoon-character cows and glowering swathes of purple autumn heather, all the time on the lookout for red-coats to cleave in two.

The English have got it wrong: it is our identification with the romantic image of Wallace that carried Braveheart to such soaring box-office success wherever Scots drew breath, not our inherent dislike of the English. That, and the healthy Scottish penchant for self-pity which, dare I admit it, raises events like Culloden 1746 and Argentina 1978 to a seminal and revered status in our collective consciousness, as opposed to single-mindedly suppressing them as the English were quick to do with Bannockburn 1314.

Compared with the popular image of Scotland, pictorial England is easier to comprehend albeit, perhaps, less rewarding: a typical southern dilettante. Her gentle countryside is haphazard, a patchwork of cities, moors and woods without obvious continuity and missing the sheer rugged, monomaniacal vastness of the Scottish Highlands. That is why the ever-practical Englishman in his intellectual straight-jacket, with his obsessive love of comforts (parasols, regattas, strawberries and cream, cucumber sandwiches), struggles with Scotland's open spaces ('what are they *for,* dear?').

And so it is with fishing. Where the English see sunny, summer chalk streams, tidy fibreglass boats, canvas stools and wicker creels, the Scots think oilskins, plus fours, wild rain-swept landscapes, leaking clinker built boats and carrier bags for the catch. While the English fishery manager goes out of his way to provide comfort for his customers, his Scottish counterpart ensures that the facilities are as spartan as possible, and takes pride in creating an assault course of concealed barbed wire and impenetrable bramble thickets that would challenge the Green Berets.

On most English fisheries, it is even possible to answer a call of nature in the seclusion of a purpose-built water closet without risking exposing a delicate part of one's anatomy to extreme air temperatures and icy hands, a hazardous operation even after years of dedicated practice. Add to that, the little casting platforms and ubiquitous wooden benches arranged at regular intervals around the bank, and you begin to understand why my childhood stereotype of the lily-livered Englishman was, if anything, reinforced when I actually came to live and fish with him.

Take that ultimate symbol of the American fly fisher, embraced with open arms by his English cousins: the fishing waistcoat. Complete with absorbent polyester mesh, ripstop nylon and front buckle closure, this peculiar item of clothing fails completely to satisfy the primary criteria of a Scottish fisherman's outer garment. It keeps its wearer neither warm nor dry. Any attempt to wear one beneath a more suitable overgarment simply renders the vital items of tackle contained within its multitudinous pockets (canted for accessibility) and attached to its various clips and springs, completely unreachable.

In an ill-fated attempt to blend in with my adopted countrymen, I did actually purchase and road test a waistcoat myself. Even allowing for its deficiencies in the field of basic climatic protection, I failed miserably to work out how the angler of average intelligence and memory capacity could ever hope to find his car keys in the 'six zippered front pockets, nine front pockets with Velcro fastenings, large zippered back pocket, full-width lower outer back pocket, two back zippered reel/spool pockets and nine internal pockets ... ' promised by the mail order catalogue.

Despite all this, the waistcoat has become an enduring testimony to the southern philosophy. Wait to see whether it's a nice day or not and, if it is, pop up to your local fishery after work, throw the waistcoat over your collar and tie, and have a cast or two. If Michael Fish was wrong and it does rain, well, you are never very far from the car and the fishing lodge offers shelter, coffee and a chance to peruse a healthy stock of flies and sundry other angling equipment.

Try as I might, I cannot get used to it. For a start, I was brought up to believe that only two climatic eventualities could ever lead to the cancellation of a fishing trip: impenetrable ice and water so high that one slip would, in all likelihood, result in the angler being fished from the North Sea by a Scandinavian trawler. Anything else was fair game and relevant only in as much as it would determine the amount of clothing worn and the degree of discomfort suffered.

Packing for a day's fishing should be a military operation, not a five minute job done before leaving for the office. Just as sitting in the car with the engine on and the radiator at maximum, sipping a hot coffee and gnawing on a day-old meat pie while the circulation slowly returns, is central to the whole fishing experience. We Scots, after all, like nothing better than a bit of self-flagellation. It makes us feel worthy and appeals to our nature, especially if it is followed by the opportunity to moan about it in the pub. That is why we make such good Trade Union leaders. Self-righteous complaint is in our Celtic blood.

And that is the nub of the problem: however I might try to dress it up, I will always be a stranger here. Being Scottish is just not a part-time thing. It does not fade like a nasty rash or wear off like growing pains, no matter how fervently you might wish it would every time the national teams visit Twickenham or the Millennium Stadium. The close confines of an English stock pond or a concrete reservoir full of windsurfers and water skiers, are to me what Burscough Town is to Glasgow Rangers. Acceptable only when nothing better is available.

Once a Scot, always a Scot.

2

THE BEST LAID PLANS

First find a prospective wife, then teach her to fish. It sounded like good advice to me and so I had laid my plans accordingly. Realising intuitively just how critical an occasion this was, I had chosen the venue carefully: a little loch up in the Skye hills which had seldom let me down. The fish were not large (a half-pounder was a good one) but they were obliging and it was a good water on which to ply the traditional wet fly. Equally important, it was a pleasant place where I could be sure we would encounter no other anglers to compromise the delicate learning process.

We had reached the lodge early to pick up the boat keys from the owner of the estate, a delightful lady who, with her husband, had settled in the glen in a different era, an era when Britain was great and the Commonwealth was an institute to be proud of. She was unfailingly generous with her hospitality and always took a genuine interest in our success.

Some time later, we parked the car in its usual spot and set out, me full of good cheer, my wife-to-be perhaps a little apprehensive. Casting in the back garden on a still afternoon was one thing but controlling three wet flies in the cramped confines of a small rowing boat with, in all probability, a strong wind blowing over her shoulders, seemed like a different proposition altogether.

We made good time over the fields and managed to cross the Drynoch, hopping from one stone to the next, without serious misadventure. It had been a dry summer and the river was low, not at all the raging torrent which had caused me so much trouble on my last visit. Further down the glen, where the Drynoch emptied into Loch Harport, the sea trout congregated frustratingly near to their destination but unable to progress any further until the rains came.

From there, it was a long, muscle-wrenching climb up the steep side of the glen through rough heather and the occasional stand of waste-high bracken. Already, the vegetation was turning brown in places, dried by the sun and lack of rain, and the ground felt springy underfoot.

As we climbed, sheltered for the time being from the wind, the sun came out and we sweated heavily beneath jerseys and Barbours. Fortunately, the spectacular view out along Loch Harport towards the straggling crofting community of Portnalong offered a good excuse for regular stops. Aching legs could be stretched surreptitiously and lungs filled with deep draughts of clean, clear air.

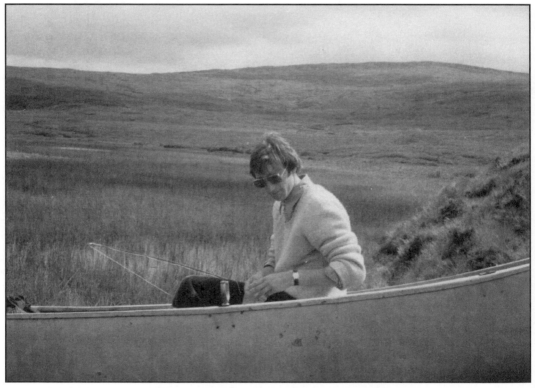

Taking a break on Loch a' Ghrobain, Skye

As we crossed the plateau towards the dip where I knew Loch a' Ghrobain was hidden, the pain of the climb was quickly forgotten, swamped by mounting excitement and anticipation. For me, working now in the deep south of England, this was the first chance in three long years to return to my beloved hill lochs.

Then, almost before we realised it, there it was, a tiny hidden world of its own, one end covered with reeds, the other open water with a steep, rocky shore. As we sat in the heather by the boat, taking in the sheer beauty and isolation, the haunting wail of a great northern diver floated soulfully across the waves. An answering call drifted on the wind from far above. Sinking deeper into the heather, I finally felt the tensions of work drain away; I was at peace with myself and the world for the first time in as long as I could remember.

With an effort, I shook myself out of my reverie; I had a mission to accomplish. Spirits high, we set forth.

But as we drifted towards the reeds, no rise to interrupt our progress, I began to wonder if my carefully laid plans might yet go awry. We had only just started our second drift, however, when my faith was rewarded and a determined little trout took hold of my pupil's bob fly as it skipped enticingly across the waves towards the boat. Looking back, I am not sure who was most surprised, the fish or my wife-to-be, but to her credit the latter recovered her composure quicker than the former. Before it could say 'Bloody Butcher', that unsuspecting trout was shooting across the surface like a motorboat and into the waiting net.

My future wife sat there, a gleam in her eye, convinced that this fishing game was much easier than I had let on. I grinned inwardly and permitted myself a mental pat on the back. Mission accomplished: clearly it was not just the venue I had chosen well!

From that day to this, my wife has been a keen fisher, albeit perhaps not as fanatical as myself. She is happiest on the hill lochs, where the fish rise freely and where fishing is fun, bereft of the seriousness that can lead to bag limits becoming the measure of a day's success.

And there can be no doubting her ability. With a short line, bob fly skimming across the crest of the waves, she can hold her own with the best, as more than one hill loch trout has since discovered. She has fished with me all over the west coast of Scotland and we make a good team. I fish a longer line while she, with no less success, tempts fish from the very shadow of the boat.

But just as there is reward in having a wife who fishes, so too danger lurks. Thoughts of fishing outings with 'the lads' are soon scotched. And since she first read about the redoubtable Miss Ballantyne and her record rod-caught salmon, I have had to listen to more than just the occasional reference to a woman's superiority in matters fishy.

So just to put the record straight, I have done some painstaking research which kills that fanciful rumour once and for all. Taking into account all the occasions that my wife and I have fished together since that day on Loch a' Ghrobain, my average catch stands at a moderate three point six; my wife, meantime, has achieved just one point six fish per rod day.

Now she, to be fair, may argue that her fish have been of superior size. Unfortunately, I have not kept a record of the weight of every fish we have caught, so that theory must remain speculation; and anyway, I am sure you will agree that quantity is more important than size.

3

HAVE ROD, WILL TRAVEL

In an age when the annual family holiday is just as likely to be spent in Miami, Florida, as Blackpool, Brighton or even Majorca, one of the least expendable items of the angler's kit must surely be the poacher's rod. Today's telescopic miracle of modern ingenuity is lighter and easier to carry than the old split cane version; it fits readily into the suitcase alongside water-wings, snorkels and sun-cream and, most important of all, it is almost undetectable to wifely eyes.

Make no mistake about it, the poacher's rod can be a life saver. How many times I wonder, have fishing husbands stared wistfully into the depths of a stream in some far off and exotic holiday destination only to be jolted into alertness by the realisation that the plump form holding its station amongst the gently swaying fronds is none other than *salmo trutta*? My wife knows that look well – and she knows where to find me when I excuse myself after dinner complaining of an urgent need for fresh air.

My first experience of fishing abroad came during my last summer at school, more years ago than I care to remember. A friend and I somehow managed to persuade the school board to part with some money to send us on a study tour of Europe. Study, I admit with more than a little twinge of guilt, could not have been further from our minds. I well remember the excitement as we sat around the kitchen table poring over a map, searching for the greatest concentration of blue marks.

At the end of the day it was a close run thing between Finland, which seemed to us more water than land, and the mountainous highlands of southern Norway. A little research at the local library unearthed mouth-watering tales of landlocked salmon in Norwegian lakes and streams and our minds were made up. The Setesdal Valley it was. And that, as it turned out, was our first mistake.

River Otra, Setesdal Valley, Norway

As the appointed day came closer, so the expectation mounted. Hours were devoted to the packing of rucksacks and the almost obsessive selection of tackle. The crossing to Kristiansand passed in a fever of anticipation and even the spectacular vistas of lower Setesdal were lost on us as we sped by. And then, finally, there we were, standing on the banks of the River Otra, the weeks of preparation and anticipation over.

In an undignified hurry that belied the traditional image of the angler at work, I cast frantically towards a particularly inviting run. Already imagining the rush of line and hearing the purr of reel, I let the fly work down towards the enticing eddy at the tail. Moments passed. Nothing happened. Mildly surprised, I repeated the process. Again, nothing.

Many casts later, two dispirited and weary anglers trekked fishless back to the hostel. Later that night, drying out around the warmth of a roaring fire, we heard the first whispers of foul deeds, of black winds from industrial Europe, winds that brought a killing rain and sounded the death knell for the local fisheries.

Perhaps it was poetic justice but I could not know then that ten years later I would find myself, a professional ecologist, sitting on a Government committee investigating the effects of acid rain, responding at last to the concerns of my Scandinavian friends.

In the years since, I have learned that a poacher's rod and a box of flies are a sure passport to the discovery of secrets often hidden from those travelling lighter. The comradeship of fishing is a universal one, and one that bridges the widest ethnic and linguistic chasms. I well remember days spent on the clear, snow-fed mountain streams of the Julian Alps in the former Yugoslavia and the Tatras Mountains of Slovakia. The rivers contained brownies of a size and spirit equalled only by their shyness. And yet my lasting memories are not of fish stalked, but rather of the warm nature and friendliness of the local people.

In particular, I remember a friend made one evening in the bar of a Slovak hotel, a local angler who was at the time indulging heavily in his other hobby: *slivovic*, the national fire-water. Now I know the tale he told is not really a fishy one (leastways not in the literal sense) but it is a good yarn and as such it merits telling.

Hunting, my new companion had begun in broken and somewhat slurred English, had until recently surpassed the gentler pastimes of fishing and skiing as the major tourist attraction in that wild and beautiful part of the country. On the occasion in question, a rich American had contacted the Slovak Tourist Board to arrange a hunting trip with the sole purpose of bagging a specimen bear. Now the lady at the Tourist Board may have known little about hunting but she did appreciate the value of the dollar to the local economy. Much effort was devoted to arranging the American's schedule and booking him in to the best hotel in the province.

It was only when the lady came to hire a guide to settle the real business of the trip that her error became apparent. She had arranged the visit to coincide with their quarry's annual hibernation.

At this point my friend broke off from his narrative and peered up at me from his bar stool, his ruddy face expectant. For a moment I stared vacantly back, then the penny dropped and I ordered another round. As he waited for the drinks to arrive, my companion deliberately and with an air of reverence, removed a beautifully tied dry fly from the rim of his hat, held it up to the light, then set it with exaggerated care on the bar in front of him. Apparently satisfied, he cleared his throat and resumed his tale.

Convinced that she had no alternative, the lady from the Tourist Board decided that the only remaining course of action was to contact her client, explain her error with a suitable display of humility, and cancel the trip. Walking home through the forest that night, brooding darkly on her misfortunes, she almost failed to notice a poster pinned to the trunk of a tree. The poster advertised a travelling circus with a performing bear as its star attraction. Even now, in her black mood of depression, the significance of this coincidence was almost lost on her. Then, all at once, a blinding flash of light cut through her musings, causing her spirits to soar wildly. Just maybe, this was the answer to her prayers!

That very night she contacted the circus and arranged, at great expense, to purchase the bear.

The weeks passed quickly and in no time at all the American arrived, spirits high in anticipation. Early on the appointed morning, hunter and guide set out, and before long spotted the first signs of bear tracks in the snow. Hours of careful stalking followed until eventually there he stood, a huge bear, magnificent in the fading afternoon light.

On his belly now, the American gentleman inched forward until he had the bear in his sights. Just as he raised the rifle to his shoulder, the bear shuffled forward a couple of paces to stand in the middle of a little forest track winding its way through the trees. Sensing that something was amiss, the huge creature rose ponderously to his hind legs and sniffed the breeze, a quizzical expression on his face.

As chance would have it, a little old lady on her way home from the village shop chose that very moment to cycle into view around the corner. Seeing the bear blocking her path, she swerved in fright, fell off her bike and fled screeching in the direction from which she had appeared. Our hunter, watching developments with mounting concern, realised that he had to act fast. Raising himself quickly to his haunches, he levelled the rifle once more. But just as his finger tightened on the trigger, the bear turned, lumbered towards the now abandoned bicycle ... and cycled off into the gloom.

My new friend sat back on his stool, downed what remained of his drink and bathed in the warm glow of acclaim emanating from the appreciative crowd gathered around the bar. Some things, I reflected through a *slivovic-*induced haze, would never change. Only a fisher could tell such a tale and expect it to be believed.

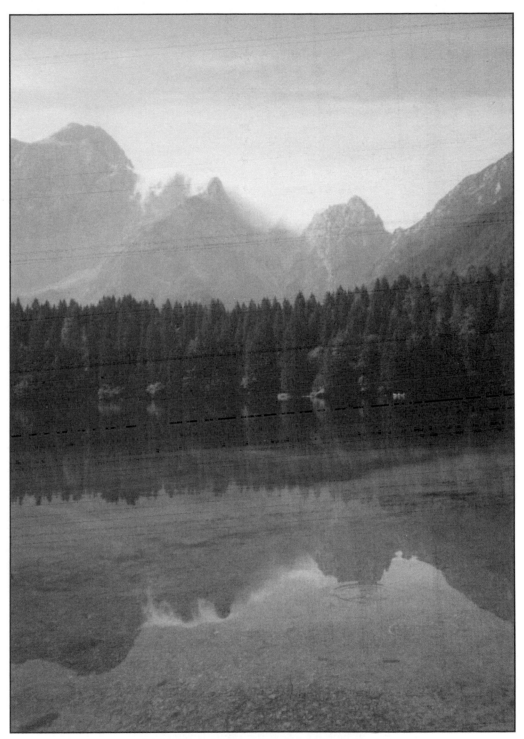

Julian Alps, Slovenia (formerly Yugoslavia)

4

LEAVING NOTHING TO CHANCE

Mid-May, my second visit to this small stock fishery and I still hadn't caught a fish. Yet the omens were good: the temperature was pleasant, a gentle breeze rippled the surface of the south reservoir, and a few mayfly danced and gyrated around the margins on feathery wings. Best of all, the occasional dorsal fin waggled briefly on the surface as a rainbow sated an appetite built over the winter months.

Yet, again, it looked like I would fail. Perhaps it was too bright, perhaps the breeze was too gentle, perhaps my flies were not sitting in the surface film the way I intended them to. Whatever the case, my carefully presented buzzers had elicited only the occasional boil, without any real evidence of serious intent.

Distractedly, I noticed an early season sedge fluttering amongst the mayfly, a drunken gatecrasher in the midst of a well-choreographed dance routine. For a moment, another rested on my arm as I cast, before recommencing its erratic journey, weaving clumsily through the cloud of graceful ephemerals. These were not the big sedge which appear later in the season to whirl maniacally across the water's surface in the gloaming but little dark flies no longer than my thumbnail with steepled wings and wonderfully delicate antennae.

It was a moment before I asked the obvious question. Were the rising trout taking buzzers after all? As the question hung for a moment unanswered, my attention was drawn to a splashy rise on the edge of the rippled water, just the sort of rise you might expect from a hungry trout on the trail of a juicy sedge.

A quick examination of the dry fly box and on went a dark deer's hair sedge. It was a touch bigger than the natural, perhaps, but otherwise similar and the best I could do. A long cast out towards the ripple and there it sat, bobbing proudly, simply daring a fish to take. A short pull on the line, just enough to make the fly twitch, and the artificial disappeared abruptly in a flurry of droplets. But the sheer thrill of the moment cut through all the careful years of schooling and I reacted like that nine year-old, long ago on the mossy banks of a little stream in Perthshire. Only the result was different.

Not for the first time, I learnt a hard lesson. What Howell Raines christened the 'Redneck Way', that ancestral urge to forget the niceties of fly fishing and simply get your fish onto the bank and into the bag, must be curbed when the angler is after large trout with light tackle. It is one of the beautiful things about fly fishing, just as it is, at the same time, one of the frustrations. The mind is required to make an almost infinitesimally rapid series of calculations and to translate these in less time than it takes to blink an eye into a balanced reaction generating precisely the right amount of force to slide the hook point home without breaking the cast or pulling the fly from the fish's mouth.

As if that action is not testing enough, the fisherman is then required to suspend his natural exuberance and do the most uncharacteristic thing of all in this moment of excitement and sheer raw power: release the pressure and surrender to the fish, allowing it to go where it will.

On this occasion, I did none of these things. I simply responded by jerking backwards with a force which might have resulted in a smaller trout taking to the air. The only surprise was that the cast did not part and that, by some stroke of undeserved fortune, the only small dark sedge I possessed, remained attached to the couple of hundred pounds worth of carefully-balanced tackle which I had abused so badly.

I did not stop to treat the fly with a further dose of floatant. In seconds, I had returned him unceremoniously to the water. Despite my lack of consideration, and thanks in no small part to the indefatigable spirit of the deer's hair, the fly still floated upright and with that same air of brazen challenge that had clearly proved so alluring moments earlier.

This time, the fly remained in place, riding the ripples for several minutes before the next rainbow happened by. Nerves steeled, I managed to control my baser instincts sufficiently long to feel, for a moment, the thump of what seemed to be a well-hooked trout, only to be followed instantaneously by the slackness that means a fish lost and the boiling frustration that numbs the angler's ability to think logically.

I suspect it was not at the forefront of my mind at the time but I might well have spent a few moments pondering Raines' observation that ' ... sliding home the hook and then bowing to the energy of the fish is easier to describe than to execute ... ' In many ways, it is fair to say that mastery of this apparently simple skill, represents the true distinction between those who are good at casting and those who are good at catching trout.

As it was, my feelings of inadequacy were expressed, not by quiet, philosophical thought but, less practically, by a few wasted moments pacing up and down the bank hurling curses into the genial and undeserving summer sky.

So much for the gentle sport.

With an effort, I calmed myself sufficiently to return to useful action, only to find to my horror, that I seemed to have sunk deep within the clutches of my very own Ground Hog Day. Time and again, fish came to the fly. Sometimes they rose short. On other occasions they took the fly with gusto and confidence. But none stuck around for long. Only the sinking sun and my increasingly colourful and desperate language, provided evidence that each was indeed a separate event and a different trout.

Strangely, and perhaps this is testimony to the sheer stubbornness of human nature, during all this adversity, I neither changed my fly nor moved along the bank. So it was not until the temperature started to drop and the rises dwindled gradually into stillness, that I discovered why I had just completed another afternoon without a fish. As I snipped the battered and bruised sedge from the end of my cast and made several abortive attempts to hook the fly into the ethafoam lining of my dry fly box, the truth sank in. The hook had snapped at the bend. Probably, I reflected ruefully, the result of that careless Redneck heave which had lost me the first fish of the day.

It had taken me forty odd years of fishing and one very hard lesson to learn to leave nothing to chance.

PART VII
WILDERNESS YEARS

For a short period in the mid eighties, fishing was rivalled in my affections by the equally gentlemanly pursuit of village cricket. In the pleasant climate of the South, where life revolved around picture-postcard pubs with big open hearths and windows onto rose-scented gardens, cricket had an air of comfortable belonging which it could never have in the austerity of the North.

In some ways too, the attractions of the two very different pastimes were remarkably similar: characters abounded in the village game, imparting to its participants a soothing antidote to the arrogance of high society Henley. For me, cricket was as much about recognising my own limitations as it was about learning techniques or playing to win. I took to it like a trout to a chalk stream and for a few golden summers I immersed myself in the camaraderie and the whole glorious atmosphere of the game. Even now, I can still smell the fresh-cut grass, and the liniment and bandages of the changing room.

Life was pleasant and for a while, at least, the fishing tackle gathered dust in a corner.

1

THE BIG MAN

I first met Big Jim in the most unlikely of places: a cosy nook in a nice respectable Henley pub. A remarkable number of my subsequent encounters with the 'Big Man' have also taken place in one drinking establishment or another, come to think of it, though not always as reputable.

I had only been in the area for a short time, so it seemed to me ironic that, for the second time in as many weeks, the first words I should hear as I waited to order a pint at this bright, cheerful bar, full to bursting with well-dressed and well-spoken people, should assume a broad accent whose origins I immediately placed as 'not far from Glasgow'.

'Where d'ye cum frae?' was his opening gambit, rapidly followed by, 'Ah'm Jim, by the way.'

The owner of this comfortingly familiar accent certainly stood out from the crowd. I found myself looking down at a short, rotund figure, red of complexion, with thick glasses and dressed in scruffy, ill-fitting jeans and t-shirt.

We exchanged pleasantries for a few moments. Then I politely excused myself and rejoined my new workmates by the window. Big Jim, I noted, followed me.

Halfway through the evening, the penny finally dropped. Big Jim was himself a research chemist at the Centre.

Our next encounter occurred a few days later. The works cricket club was having a trial for potential players. I had not played cricket since school days, some dozen years before, but I followed the game avidly and I was desperately keen to get involved in the works' social scene. So I had put my name forward as soon as I had seen the notice.

Clearly, Big Jim had designs on the works' team too. When I arrived at the ground, there he was standing on the boundary rope shouting staccato

Henley-on-Thames, more famous for rowing than cricket

instructions to all and sundry (none of whom showed any obvious sign of listening), cricket whites bursting at the seams like a cross between the redoubtable David Shepherd and Elvis in the latter stages of his career.

As it happened, the game was great fun and a roaring success. I scored enough runs, more, I suspect, by luck than judgement, to get myself into the team. The real highlight of the evening, however, was an interesting spell of spin bowling delivered by Big Jim himself.

Now Big Jim was not built for bowling. Getting his arm over at all was an achievement; bowling accurately was virtually impossible. Big Jim's two overs took so long to complete that the match barely finished before the moon rose over the Dog and Badger. His eventual figures were: two overs, no maidens, no wickets for forty-five runs (thirty of which were wides, the more exotic of these failing even to land on the square).

The following day, I bumped into Big Jim in the corridor at work. Far from being chagrined, Big Jim informed me proudly that he had been quite satisfied with his performance.

'It's a shame,' he intoned enthusiastically, 'that the wicket wasnie takin spin.'

I carefully refrained from pointing out that it had been difficult to assess what the wicket was taking, seeing as the ball had rarely come into contact with it.

Big Jim also turned out occasionally for the local village side, usually when we were short of a player or two. The side played on a poplar-fringed ground high on a hill overlooking the Thames valley, surrounded by rich pasture. Occasionally, an unusually exuberant hit over mid-wicket would deposit the ball right in the midst of a neighbouring field of cows.

During one match, we had noticed a rather surly looking bull in residence, presumably there to perform his allotted bovine task. Big Jim was fielding on the boundary out of harm's way when the opposition batsman, who had been tied down for some time, unleashed a mighty and uncharacteristically flamboyant blow which cleared Big Jim comfortably to land right in the midst of a knot of quietly grazing cows.

Never a man to shirk his duty, Big Jim, with much panting, mounted the fence to retrieve the ball. For the bull, no doubt bored by a surfeit of female company, the opportunity to do mischief was clearly too much to resist. Eyeing Big Jim ominously and pawing the ground with one mighty hoof, he began to amble, slowly at first but with gathering pace, towards the now rapidly retreating figure in white.

Big Jim moved remarkably quickly for a man of his size (quicker, some wag pointed out, than he had ever done between the wickets). His escape seemed assured until, in his haste, he attempted to pull his trailing leg over the topmost strand of barbed wire. There followed a clearly audible ripping sound accompanied by a rumbling expletive. Big Jim was stuck like a fly to

fly-paper. Any pretence of decorum on the part of Big Jim's fellow cricketers crumbled at this point. Ten fielders, two batsmen, and two umpires collapsed to the ground as one man, in the grip of helpless mirth, while Big Jim sat there returning the bull's glare, and uttering a string of loud obscenities hardly consistent with the peaceful and gentlemanly image of the great game. Eventually, it was the lone spectator who recovered his senses sufficiently to effect a rescue.

I have since had the pleasure of playing cricket with Big Jim on many an occasion. His optimism is wonderfully unquenchable. Never once have I seen him lose patience with his own lack of success or physical limitations. Big Jim plays cricket for just one reason: he plays because he enjoys playing. And in doing so, he shames many a more talented player, moody and petulant in failure, arrogant and overbearing in success.

Big Jim does hold one record which is worthy of an entry in the *Guinness Book of Records,* if not perhaps the hallowed pages of *Wisden*. Big Jim is the only player, to my knowledge, who has ever retired injured having twisted an ankle on the way out to bat ...

2

ON THE ANALYST'S COUCH

Like many sports, fishing is fertile ground for those with a bent towards psychology. Indeed, the more I fish, the more convinced I become that success owes as much to what goes on in the angler's head as it does to what happens beneath the water's surface: an interesting hypothesis, perhaps, for a student of the human mind.

Our student might do well to start by asking why it should be that I catch fish on a size sixteen March Brown Spider on the middle dropper, when my fishing companion, using the same tactics from the same boat, catches his on a size ten Peter Ross on the point? To confound the mystery, persuade him to switch to a little March Brown Spider and you can be sure he will stop catching fish.

Of course it may all come down to some subtle and completely subconscious difference in the way we work our flies. On the other hand, it seems much more likely that I catch fish on the March Brown Spider because I fish it with complete confidence. The Peter Ross has never caught me fish, inspires in me no confidence whatsoever and now rarely sees the light of day unless I am thoroughly desperate. In such a scenario, of course, it is even less likely to succeed.

On our reservoirs, in particular, is it really surprising that certain lures go through cycles of intense and unrivalled popularity? All it takes is for the Cat's Whisker to catch a few fish on a day when perhaps any fly of similar size or colour would have performed equally well. Up goes 'Cat's Whisker' on the blackboard, while in the fishery hut it is the subject of many a whispered piece of sage advice. Lo-and-behold, the very next day, only the Cat's Whisker catches fish. The process, of course, is self-perpetuating, feeding on the predictability of human nature and the continual, self-imposed pressure to play safe, to conform.

One only has to dabble in the angling press to see that anglers, like the rest of society, are susceptible to fashion. If Bob Church says that the High Rise Doll is the fly to catch fry feeders, then what do we all go out and buy when the rainbow trout are splashing around with abandon in the shallows? Does anyone remember the Chenille Doll, that peculiar invention resembling nothing as much as an old-fashioned pipe cleaner, or the Dog Nobbler or, come to that, the Missionary? All languish in my fly box unused in years, yet all were 'essential' parts of the reservoir angler's armoury in their day.

And what of the Whiskey Fly, that bright orange contraption which looks as if it might be more at home under the strobe lights of a fashionable disco, than hooked in the rim of a battered old deerstalker? I am in no position to cast the first stone because I was one of the many who bought a dozen, convinced that a fly which looked so good and came so highly recommended had to be the answer to all my piscatorial prayers. But like all 'never-fail' flies, ultimately it did just what it was not supposed to do: it failed.

In the case of the Whiskey Fly, however, at least it had its brief moment of glory on the delightful Loch Monzievard, undoubtedly one of the most beautiful managed fisheries that I have ever had the pleasure to fish. Monzievard is sheltered, dotted with pretty little tree-clad islands and nestles deep in the midst of mixed pine and broad-leaved woodland. On a sunny day, the varied shades of green, from dark Scots pine to pale beech and lime, make a glorious patina as they are reflected in the loch's gentle face. Later in the year, the riot of russets, yellows and golds creates a fiery and splendid backdrop reminiscent of the finest autumn day in New England.

Monzievard also contains a fascinating mixture of wild brown trout, stocked rainbows and American brook trout. The latter, we discovered, had established a breeding population in the loch, quite an unusual phenomenon in this country but a fitting tribute to the uniqueness of the location.

We had fished Monzievard regularly that summer from my friend's home base in Bridge of Allan and had really begun to get to grips, or so we thought, with the loch and its mysteries. But as in life, whenever you think you have finally cracked it, that is when you are due for a fall.

I had caught a rainbow fairly early on, fishing a Red Tag along the bottom in the shallow water behind our favourite little island. Here, we had discovered, voracious rainbows were wont to gorge themselves on a rich diet of snail and shrimp. Strangely, that was where our luck had ended. As the day progressed and a sporadic rise developed, I became more and more frustrated. Suddenly, all the techniques which had brought us fish all summer long simply would not work.

Swiping at a wasp that buzzed irritatingly around the boat, I changed my cast for the umpteenth time. But still, the answer eluded me. Close to giving up, I took recourse to the ultimate action. I reeled in and set about plundering the sandwich box. The world always looked better after a cup of coffee and one of my favourite bacon sandwiches, the bacon done until it was just starting to burn.

As soon as I opened the picnic box, another wasp settled on the lid, no doubt hopeful of a share in my lunch. Cursing, I brushed it away with a force which sent it spinning onto the water a yard or two from the boat. Out of the corner of my eye, I detected a movement and looked up just in time to see my erstwhile luncheon companion disappear in a swirl of fin and sparkling flank.

At last the penny dropped.

Of course my excitement was short-lived; it took me only scant moments to discover that likely wasp imitations did not exactly feature large in my fly box. Fighting off despair, my eyes settled in desperation on the long-ignored Whiskey Fly. Now the Whiskey Fly looks about as much like a wasp when you scrutinise it closely as the next fly, but it is bright, it is garish and it did give me a spark of much-needed hope.

On it went, bacon sandwiches forgotten for the time being. And sure enough, on my second cast, there was a confident swirl and I was into a nice rainbow, my second of the day.

At this point I am sure it is not beyond the imagination to anticipate the rest of my tale. Confidence suddenly restored, I could not fail. Within half an hour, I had five fish in the boat and my companion, equally unsuccessful up to this point but quick to capitalise on my fortuitous discovery, had seven. At various stages of the afternoon, we even played fish simultaneously.

For the rest of that season the Whiskey Fly was abruptly raised to the exalted status of favourite. I felt confident fishing it; it was a regular part of the starting line-up and, not surprisingly, it responded by catching the odd fish or two, albeit never in the quantity of that memorable day on Loch Monzievard. Since that season, however, I have never caught another trout on the fly, even on the rare occasion when wasps have again swarmed in numbers. Now, many years later, it sits in my fly box from one season to the next, untouched.

The test of a truly great fly, of course, is its ability to catch sufficient fish over an extended period to give the angler that feeling of confidence every time he ties it to the end of his cast. Despite the occasional brief and torrid affair with some new and beguiling creation, when the going gets tough, I have always returned to a select dozen or so flies like an errant husband returning home to the familiar comforts of wife and family.

Neither, I am sure, would it improve my brother anglers' chances of success to know what flies these are. I strongly suspect that what works for me would not work for anyone else.

As our student psychologist probes deeper still into the dark corners of his subject's psyche, other evidence might emerge to support his theory that all is not what it seems.

How many times I wonder, often in the middle of the slowest of days, has the angler received from nowhere that subliminal signal which suddenly makes the heart quicken and stops the mind from its wandering? Should he try to analyse the feeling, any meaningful explanation slips through the fingers like so many grains of sand. Yet sure enough, within seconds, a fish rises or the line tightens.

This heightening of the senses, for such is the only explanation I can suggest, is an integral part of fishing which manifests itself in many ways. I could not count the number of times I have stood on a bridge with a friend who does not fish and pointed excitedly to the gently waving shape, patrolling the edge of the weed bed as he picks up the occasional nymph borne downstream on the current. I might see him clear as day and yet the response from my companion is predictable in its inevitability: 'Where? I can't see a thing.' Half an hour later, I have frequently begun to suspect myself of hallucinating or my friend of malicious trickery.

And then there are the psychological changes which occur as the angler matures, leaving behind forever the phase when success is measured in numbers or pounds and ounces. It is always nice to catch fish; that, after all, is what fishing is about. But as the years roll by, the simple pleasures of being there, of casting a nice line, grow to outweigh the less esoteric and more results-oriented goals of the novice. Eventually, the angler needs nought but the occasional fish to keep the interest going.

That too, is part of the rich psychological tapestry which our student must unravel before his thesis is finally complete.

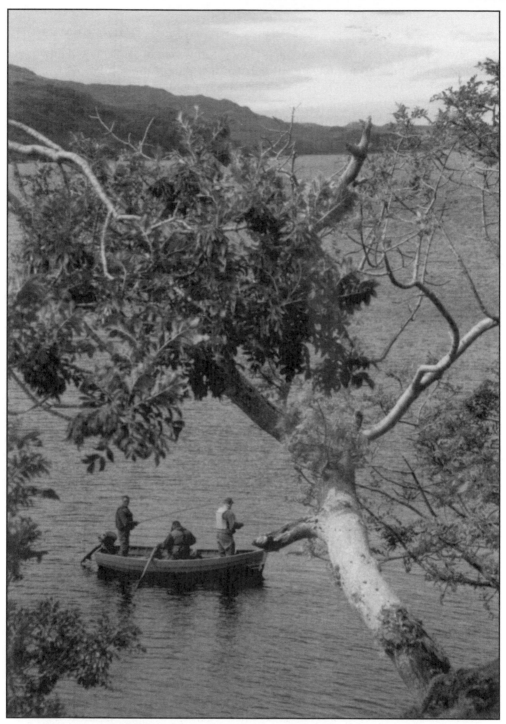

'Do you ever get the feeling you're being watched?' A quiet corner on Loch Assynt, Sutherland

3

EACH TO HIS OWN

Inever much cared for climbing. The way I look at it, you can generally see the top of a mountain from the bottom, so why go through the painful experience of hauling one foot after the other all the way to the top just to confirm what you already know? And if ever you do suddenly develop an inexplicable urge to stand on the top of a high peak, choose your peak carefully and there will be cable cars or chair lifts to get you there.

Perhaps I am biased but if I am, it is probably with good reason.

I once went on a 'rambling holiday' in the Alps. At least that is how the brochure described it and, in fairness, that is how it started out. However, it was not long before a 'gentle stroll with leisurely stop for lunch' (which conjured up images of sunshine and tavernas with stripy awnings) had turned into more of a 'forced march on survival rations', while 'the occasional slight gradient' had mysteriously metamorphosed into 'Triglav, the highest peak in Yugoslavia, with overnight stop in climbing hut'. This was most definitely not what I had in mind when I made the booking.

Not surprisingly, I soon got fed up. Fed up with sore feet, fed up with bursting lungs and, most of all, fed up with hour upon monotonous hour, gazing unwaveringly at the taut, leathery calf muscles a few inches in front of my nose. I like to think I am a fairly tolerant sort of person but everyone has his limits. I rebelled, cut my losses and turned the remaining days into a fishing/eating/drinking holiday in the company of a few like-minded individuals. To this day, my only regret was that it took me so long to make the break.

We fishers can get a reputation for being a touch eccentric but believe me, we have nothing on the climbing fraternity. A more dedicatedly masochistic bunch I have never come across. In appearance, my erstwhile Alpine companions resembled nothing as much as a tribe of gnarled gnomes, all craggy wind-burnt faces and bobble hats, with painfully rough looking tweed plus-fours and calves the size of bull's thighs (and that includes the ladies). For three solid days, we climbed up one mountain and down the next like the Grand Old Duke of York's foot soldiers, largely oblivious to the scenery and the wonders of nature all around us, stopping only long enough to consume our meagre packed lunches and consult map and compass in the coldest, most windswept spots our leader could locate.

The content of our lunch boxes told its own story. It did not vary: a single pork chop inserted between two dry slices of bread and a couple of nondescript biscuits. The very austerity of the picnic fare seemed to me typical of the whole experience. When I go fishing, I take great pride in lunch. The day would simply not be complete without a couple of these nice little pies from the delicatessen's counter at the local supermarket (you know the ones), a bacon sandwich or two, and perhaps a *pakora* or other spicy little sweet meat, with a generous slice of cake and some biscuits and cheese to finish. In short, a decent picnic intended for consumption in leisurely fashion while contemplating the peace, the quiet and the countryside alone, or alternatively enjoying a lively discussion about life, the universe and spiralling house prices with a like-minded companion.

Balancing precariously astride a narrow Alpine ridge, unable to take my eye off the pork chop for fear of another bout of debilitating vertigo, while wolfing my meagre ration so as not to get left behind, is not really my idea of a stimulating lunch break to look forward to or to bolster flagging spirits. And when the conversation is limited to how many metres you can manage before evening falls and to the precise location of that little plaque commemorating the Norwegian climber who plunged to his death in weather, come to think of it, remarkably like this … well, I am afraid the pork chop sandwich tends to stick in the gullet somewhat.

When it comes to fishing, I am not ashamed to admit that if I can hitch an argocat ride (not a regular occurrence unfortunately), or get the car a few hundred yards along the rough track towards the loch, I will do it, no questions asked. But make no mistake about it, if a loch reputed to contain good trout with a willing disposition lies over the next ridge, I will get there and get there faster than most, in complete defiance of aching limbs, sweating brow and laboured breathing. It is one thing toiling up a near-vertical gradient simply because it is there: quite another striding purposefully across the moors, with the possibility of a beautiful loch and a fine trout at the other end.

To reach many of the lochs I have fished, and some of those I have written about, has entailed, in retrospect, mind-bogglingly lengthy return trips anything up to fourteen miles in total, not to mention the additional mileage clocked up during the course of an average day's fishing. And, of course, distance always seems much greater on the ground than on the map, particularly over rough ground with knee-high heather and treacherous peat bogs to negotiate, where each successive ridge seems only to give way to another. On such days, I have often reached my destination so tired as to feel almost unable to cast a line, never mind launch and row a heavy boat. Yet it is amazing how quickly the tiredness can disappear given a promising breeze and the odd splashing trout. Just as the long walk home can seem impossible even to contemplate, until that is, there are fishy tales begging to be told over a good meal and a cold beer.

In some ways, my fishing outlook is, I suspect, just an extension of my attitude to life and certainly entirely consistent with my sporting philosophy. All these painful and mind-numbingly boring hours in the gym pumping irons and pounding the treadmill just so that you can dream of beating your opponent on the squash court all seem somewhat distasteful, especially when you know full well that your adversary is actually a much better player than you are. So I avoid that if I can. When, at the end of a long, hot summer of over-indulgence, a few weeks of pain are necessary to extend my playing career by another season, well, so be it, but I will do my work on the squash court, not in the gym.

We modern men are, of course, very good at the art of self-deception. I tell myself that mine is a noble and dignified philosophy. Yet all the while, I suspect that it is also a philosophy which might not bear close scrutiny. Somehow, I find it irritatingly hard to shake the conviction that, in reality, I am just plain lazy …

Either way, my Alpine experience acted as a timely reminder that, for me at least, there was no substitute for fishing.

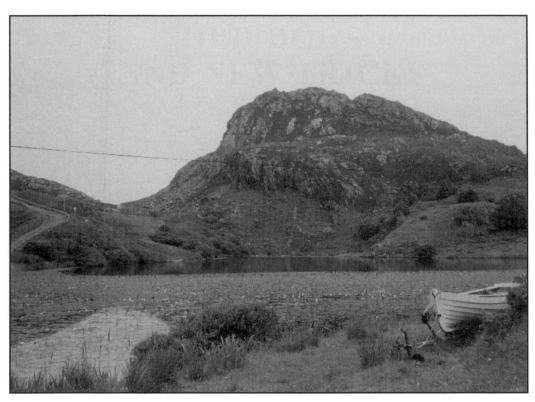

A still day on a small Irish lough, County Cork, Eire

PART VIII
LIES, DAMN LIES AND STATISTICS

I returned briefly to Scotland towards the end of the eighties to work for a firm of consultants in Aberdeen. It was while living there that I got married.

I found Aberdeen a strange city. French or American accents were as common on Union Street on a Saturday afternoon as the tangy, descriptive dialogue of the native Aberdonian tongue. It was a city of quirky contrasts, brash and reserved by turns. You could jump on a flight to Norway as easily as a Londoner might catch a tube to Green Park, yet the cultural highlights of our stay were concerts featuring Isla St Clair (remember Larry Grayson's side-kick on the 'Generation Game'?) and Jethro Tull, the ultimate throwback to the sixties. When the rather more current Suzanne Vega appeared briefly, the wicked rumour quickly did the rounds that her agent had mistakenly assumed it was Aberdeen, Alabama, when accepting the booking.

Perhaps it is inevitable that my view of Aberdeen was a touch jaundiced. The thrills of returning to Scotland, of marriage and of owning my first home were largely overwhelmed by a job I loathed where the 'bottom line' was everything and by a dawning realisation that the idealism I had shared as a student with my contemporaries was eroding just as surely as my hairline was beginning to recede.

When I was made redundant with just a week's notice, the writing was on the wall. It had been a brief return 'home'.

1

SOLACE
BY THE WATERSIDE

It was a cold, grey day, mirroring exactly my state of mind. Inside, I felt numbed and empty: I could not even find it within myself to worry or panic. I reflected bitterly on the irony or crass stupidity that had caused me to leave the South and travel here for a job which had been little more than an illusion. The hope and optimism of youth seemed a long way off. I stuck another imaginary pin in a smugly grinning effigy of the Iron Lady. But the cold defiance in her eyes only glittered the more strongly.

In a mixture of despair and anguish, I kicked at a branch lying where it had fallen in the recent gales, sending it spinning along the pavement and into the gutter. I kept walking. No destination. No plan.

We could not possibly pay the mortgage. So where would we live? And how would we get there when the keys to my company car were relinquished? I had no answers. I only knew that it would take time. That nothing would be solved today. For now, it seemed more productive to focus on revenge.

Turning my attention from Westminster to more realistic targets, I grinned bleakly at the prospect of the gleeful call I could make when the car sat on the moors with no petrol in the tank. Then I wondered how I would get home.

A little later, I sat with a long coffee, staring through the condensation that ran in little rivers down the windows of the café. Across the promenade, the waves pounded incessantly at the sea wall, representing a permanence that I did not feel. Round the headland, a small fishing boat struggled into view, making slow progress into the teeth of the wind. I felt a brief empathy with its crew, fighting for their living in a dying industry. Forced inexorably to their knees when all around the affluence of the oil industry was flaunted so brazenly. Two communities making a living from the sea: one of the past, one of the here and now.

In the midst of this unremitting gloom, I had my first positive thought since being summoned to sit in line and wait for my turn to face the Board. For the time being at least, I still had the car and a few pounds in the bank account. One of the attractions of life in the North East had always been the fishing. Until now I had been working so hard trying to keep someone else's business afloat that I had taken little advantage of our location.

Immediately, the clouds lifted and I felt, if not optimism, at least the germ of defiance. I would not go to work tomorrow. I would drive down the coast to the little fishery which I had passed in a hurry so many times before, cock a snook at the Chief Executive, laugh in the face of the Head of Finance, and seek my own solace.

And that's how I came, at last, to fish on this little loch high on the cliffs looking out over the white-flecked North Sea. In truth, I did little real fishing. Much of the time my mind was blank as I let the strong smell of the sea fill my nostrils and the sharp cries of the herring gulls resonate inside my head. Despite my inattention, I believe I did catch one or two fish. Much more important, I revelled in that sense of life and power that had been so diminished by recent happenings. I felt the healing powers of the environment mending hurts. I felt the soothing rhythm of the cast and the raw energy of hooked trout.

Perhaps I felt a little sympathy too for others locked into the unending cycle of working and striving for betterment without recourse to this escape. Finally, I let go of just a little of the bitterness and hatred. The CEO was welcome to his Company and his power games. I was stronger, I would find a new future.

And wherever that future was, there would be waters to fish and fish to catch.

2

TRAMPS, CONSTABLES AND BIG GAME

Fishing is as much about people as it is about fish, not just the people one fishes with but the characters who flit briefly in and out of an angling life leaving it immeasurably enriched by the experience.

Those readers burdened by the misfortune of birth south of Hadrian's Wall will undoubtedly be party to that greatest of all myths about the Scots, that which attributes to us a thrifty nature. Albeit from a somewhat biased standpoint, I can dispel this myth once and for all; there are, in fact, no more generous people on God's Earth. Yet despite its inaccuracy, this stereotypic characteristic more than any other has left its indelible mark on a nation's psyche. Whenever the next round needs buying, it is the Scot who feels the greatest pressure to show willing. If I did not know better, I might be tempted to suggest that the very creation and perpetuation of the myth was, in fact, a calculated ploy designed to achieve just that end ...

Leaving my national prejudices to one side, however, it is true to say that within every nation (be it Scotland, England or Outer Mongolia) there is certain to be one locale more than any other whose people have become the butt of such eccentric jokes. The tale that follows was first related to me by an Aberdonian during a lull in activity on the banks of the Don. Only the origins of the tale absolve my feelings of guilt at recounting it here. The ability to laugh at oneself is a gift indeed.

There once was a tramp, or so the story goes, who passed his days hiking the length and breadth of Britain seeking shelter when and where he could find it: without doubt, a solitary and rough existence. But our friend was well versed in the wiles of survival. Whenever the going got really tough, he had a card up his sleeve which never failed to deliver solace. First, he would find himself a field of cows, not generally a difficult task in rural Britain, then he would locate what might, in polite circles, be referred to as a cow-pat. Burdened with this unsavoury item, he would head for the nearest farmhouse with all haste.

On reaching the front door, the hero of our tale would pause just long enough to compose himself, expertly transforming healthy, weather-beaten features until he looked every bit as tired and ill-fed as a street urchin from some Dickensian poor house. This metamorphosis he had perfected in a manner reminiscent of Olivier or Burton at the height of their powers.

When the farmer's wife appeared at the door, our friend would deliver his master-stroke. Shoulders hunched, eyes glued to feet, he would hold the cow-pat up for inspection, begging the poor, beguiled woman for a pinch of salt to make it more palatable. This masterful tactic had proved infallible, leading invariably to a hot meal and a seat by the hearth.

On one such occasion, the tramp had reached the outskirts of Aberdeen on the northerly part of his annual migration. The last storms of winter were ripping in from the Arctic, ice thick on rivers and ground hard with frost. What better time to forget the rigours of the road and while away a few hours eating rabbit pie and warming numb toes by a roaring fire?

In such dire weather, however, the cows were confined to the shelter of the byre, so the only cow-pats in the pasture were dry and shrivelled, months old at best. No matter, all the easier to carry in hands blue with cold.

It did not take our friend long to locate the farmhouse and in minutes he was standing, all forlorn, on the front step. Inspired by genuine discomfort, the pinched face and desperate expression were, for once, not entirely an act. Hearing the feeble knock on the heavy oak panelled door, the farmer's wife appeared, wiping flour-covered hands on apron, cheeks all aglow from the warmth of the kitchen.

Mouth watering in anticipation of the meal that surely awaited, the tramp held his prize up for inspection with a practised gesture of supplication. As anticipated, the woman's face radiated pity and concern:

'Och, ye poor wee soul', said she, voice heavy with sympathy, 'come awa' roon' the back and I'll gie ye a fresh un.'

On another occasion, while fishing one of the beautiful machair lochs of Uist, my wife and I had our curiosity piqued as we watched what appeared to be the local police constable poking inquisitively around a little ruined bothy not far from the shore. The fishing was somewhat less than riveting that day.

When we finished for the afternoon and tied the boat up to the mooring post, the solitary figure was still there. Seeing us disembark, the constable strode purposefully over, introduced himself in a manner which left no doubt as to his importance and treated us, in lilting west Highland brogue, to an intriguing helping of local gossip. As he continued his rambling monologue, I found myself reflecting on how dull life was back home in suburbia.

At length, we managed to guide the conversation to the subject of our new friend's current investigation. Pondering just long enough to give the impression of modesty, he soon launched with thinly disguised relish into a tale of epic dimensions through which our hero strode like some latter-day colossus, combining, at one and the same time, the mental agility of Holmes and the all-action heroics of Starsky and Hutch.

To cut a long story short, our hero had single-handedly traced the baddies to the aforementioned bothy, which he now revealed with a flourish to be the site of an illicit still. Taking my cue from his dramatic pause and careful to feign suitable humility in the face of this exemplary piece of investigative brilliance, I asked our man how he had reached his stunning conclusion.

'Weel', he said, scratching his chin for a long moment and consulting his notepad, 'when I took a close look inside the building, I discovered the evidence: six empty gin bottles, twelve vodka bottles, twenty beer cans, nine whisky bottles … '

The inventory went on for some time, until, at last, the evidence was exhausted. There followed a theatrical pause to emphasise the sheer brilliance of the deductive reasoning, then Holmes finally delivered his hypothesis to an audience rapt with attention:

'Considering the evidence, I came to the conclusion that there must have been some drinking going on … '

Ah, the beauty of understatement. That night we drove the whole way back to the hotel with smiles never far from our lips, all thoughts of empty creels banished.

Of course, Scotland does not have a monopoly on characters.

Not long after my wife and I got married, we put aside for a while the worries of mortgages and unsteady jobs, and took ourselves off to spend a few days on the Kenyan coast near Malindi, a haven for big game fishermen attracted from all over the world by promises of record breaking marlin and sailfish.

Wherever we went during our visit we seemed fated to bump into a certain Yorkshire family. They, I hasten to add, were not in Kenya for the fishing. In fact, why they were there was a question which exercised our minds continually. Whenever we were unable to dodge into a convenient doorway quickly enough to avoid them, we were treated to an interminable litany of grouses and moans.

The family comprised Mum, Dad and eleven-year old son (an only child), each as Yorkshire as haggis is Scottish. Sitting by the pool, in knee length khaki shorts, socks, broad-brimmed hats and shirts buttoned up to the collar, they made us think of nothing as much as a family of overweight, grouchy warthogs.

Having got as far as Kenya, we desperately wanted to go on safari. Money, however, was short; we had spent all we had (more than all we had, in fact) getting to Africa in the first place. The compromise was a trip to Tsavo East, rising before first light, taking a long Landrover ride inland, spending a day in the park and then returning to the hotel after dark that same day. An exhausting schedule and not what we really had in mind but the only option if we were to satisfy a lifetime's ambition without putting ourselves into debt for the rest of our days.

We retired early the night before, not even waiting to swap fishy tales in the bar, as was our usual practice. Sleep, however, did not come easily, the sheer excitement of the morrow's prospects was too much for active minds. When the hands of the alarm finally reached the magical hour, we were awake, rucksacks at the ready and in the hotel foyer before you could say 'hippopotamus'.

That was when we received our first surprise. There, slouched in a line along the low wall, were the Warthogs. As we arrived, Mr Warthog announced loudly but to no one in particular:

'Ah need mah sleep, ya knows ...'

And really, that set the tone for the day. While our jaws hung open in genuine wonder at the beauty of Tsavo and at the crocodile, antelope, zebra, giraffe and buffalo that abounded on her red plains and by her waterholes, the Warthog family did nothing but grouch, moan and complain. Through it all, our Kenyan driver maintained an unruffled demeanour, grinning broadly at us as a family of real warthog crossed the road hurriedly in front of our vehicle, stopping on the far side to stare back with comical belligerence. Did he, we wondered, share our private joke?

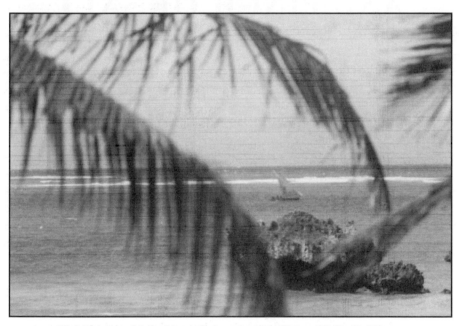

Fishing the old-fashioned way: native dhow, Malindi, Kenya

By the end of the day, we were tired but so thrilled by the sights and sounds that had assailed our senses in rapid succession, that we could barely stop talking and marvelling. As we climbed down at last from the dusty Landrover, backs stiff, eyes gritty and sore, I turned to wish the Warthogs goodnight. Mr Warthog fixed me with beady eyes which glared from the depths of sun-reddened face:

'Bloo-deh disgress-full', he spat the words out as if to rid himself of a particularly nasty taste, 'ah've seen mawr lions in 'Uddersfield, I 'ave.'

Ah well, I thought, you can't please all the people all the time.

3

ROD, REEL
AND PINCH OF SALT

Never believe what you read, I mused, not for the first time in the last few hours. It was by no means a hot day, but my shirt clung damply to my back and the occasional bead of sweat ran down my forehead and along the bridge of my nose, leaving the taste of salt on my lips. Looking back across the moors from my vantage point, I could just identify the distant figure of my wife toiling slowly towards me through knee-deep heather.

'The Goblin' (Loch a' Ghobhainn in Gaelic), could be reached in 'a brisk hour and a half from the hotel' or so the article had said. I grimaced at the memory. Already the hotel seemed vague and distant. We had left three hours ago, bolstered by a big breakfast, ready for a brisk stroll and a good day's fishing.

From where I sat on the crest of the ridge, I could make out An Ghobhainn in the distance, protected by the ominous rocky bulk of the Magician. The Magician looked suitably mysterious today, weaving his arcane spells behind a shroud of swirling mist and cloud.

With a sigh, I shouldered the rucksack, retrieved net and rods from the heather, and headed on down the slope, legs moving loosely now, as if by their own volition. Ten minutes later and I stood on Loch a' Ghobhainn's shores, exhaustion lifting a touch as I took in the healthy breeze ruffling the Goblin's dark waters. Conditions, at least, could not have been better.

Depositing the gear unceremoniously on a shingle beach, I started along the bank to find the boat. Walking from one bay to the next, however, the frustration began to mount. Why had the boat been beached so far along the shore? Would we ever get down to the real business of the day?

Then suddenly, I heard it. The unmistakable 'chug, chug' of an outboard. Screwing up my eyes against the breeze, I peered out across the waves. 'So remote', the article had confidently assured me, 'that you won't see another human being from one day to the next'. My ears had not deceived me, a boat (and it could only be the hotel boat) puttered slowly towards me, one figure manning the outboard, while another minded the two heavy rods protruding, one from either side.

As the boat executed a slow turn, bringing it to within a few hundred yards of the shore, I waved my arms strenuously to attract the occupants' attention. The two figures returned my wave, mockingly it seemed, and continued their slow troll back towards the far bank.

By now, my wife had reached the loch and was perched atop a large boulder looking quizzically along the bank to where I stood. Irritation etched on my face and, no doubt, showing clearly in the set of my shoulders, I strode back to join her. While I took deep breaths in an effort to calm myself, my wife, practical to the end, settled back in the heather and opened the lunch box.

The next twenty minutes passed uneasily as we waited for the boat's unhurried progress to bring it once more in our direction. As we sat there, my initial anger began to give way to trepidation. Poachers would not take kindly to interruption. And what if they just continued to ignore us?

In desperation, I cupped my hands and bellowed at the top of my voice in the general direction of the approaching boat. In the distance, the cloud roiled angrily around the Magician's grim flanks. Our host was not accustomed to such rude interruptions. Involuntarily, I shivered.

This time, however, my desperate tactics seemed to work. Scant moments later, two burly individuals with unmistakably local accents stepped onto the gravel bar and hauled the boat ashore. They, or so the story went, had assumed that no one was out from the hotel that day; after all, hotel fishers would have been on the water much earlier. And, yes, of course they had the hotelier's permission to use his boat.

Intuitively, I bit my tongue and decided not to argue. Instead, I asked in a tight voice where they intended to leave their outboard. The larger of the two looked at me for a long moment and then addressed me in a tone which he might have reserved for the village idiot. He had carried the outboard to the loch (how else?) and would carry it back. I decided that discretion had probably been a wise choice …

Having seen off the competition, I am happy to say that our day improved. The very first drift produced three beautifully marked trout to Soldier Palmers danced across the crest of the waves. The takes, when they came, were wild, slashing affairs, heart-stopping in their suddenness. When we left a couple of hours later, we had ten fine fish between us to ease the long walk home.

Of course that day on Loch a' Ghobhainn was only one example.

If you frequent the lowland waters, there is no need to rely on the writings of fishing journalists. There are fishery managers to advise you, log books to consult, even photos pinned to the walls of the fishing hut to testify to achievements past. But often, the only guide to the selection of the right hill loch from thousands is an article in the press or an entry in some obscure and out-of-date fishing guide.

'The fish average three-quarters of a pound' is hardly the stuff of great literary genius but it has nevertheless inspired me on many occasions. When exhaustion has set in and there is still another ridge to drag weary, city-softened legs beyond, it is such claims which give the resolve to go on.

More times than I would care to remember, I have left the loch hours later, having returned fish after fish, none of which would fill even the smallest of frying pans. Perhaps it is the fish taken which average three-quarters of a pound and several hundred fingerlings have been returned for each one killed. Or maybe I am wrong to seek a logical explanation at all; perhaps such blatant exaggeration is symptomatic of a fertile imagination. After all, on such remote lochs there is often no one to dispute the facts.

Suffice it to say that I am still waiting for the day when the fish I catch are bigger than the fish I read about!

And although the angler frequenting the hill lochs is particularly susceptible to the perils of creative writing, it can pay to be wary of the written word no matter where you fish. I wonder how often trout have been caught on a fly called the Yellow Professor. I once read that this pattern, tied on a small treble, was infallible on the Aberdeenshire Don. With a trip to that water imminent, I was banging on the door of my local tackle shop ordering a dozen almost before I had finished reading the article. And yet it was not until I had removed the aforesaid abomination from my cast in sheer exasperation, that I landed my first Don trout.

Or perhaps, when reading a particularly imaginative article, my fellow angler has, like me, raised a sceptical eyebrow when the author's reel begins to 'chatter' or a monstrous fish takes his fly 'with a bang'? Maybe I am the exception that proves the rule but I cannot remember ever hooking a talking trout which has exploded on impact!

So the moral of this yarn is clear. Enjoy the musings of piscine storytellers but, when the real business of the season begins, do not rely too much on the meanderings of others. Be the author of your own tales.

4

A TALE OF TWO GHILLIES

Once upon a time, on neighbouring estates in the hills not far from Loch Ness, there lived two ghillies: Angus and Alastair. Now each was a fine ghillie in his own right, skilled at finding the best salmon lie and selecting the right fly. But, in all other respects, the two were as different as chalk from cheese.

Angus was a hard drinking cynic, not averse to a little tactical cheating where it was necessary to please his client and to catch fish. When the tips were good, Angus' evenings were spent in the public bar, where he would entertain the younger ghillies with raucous stories of exaggerated exploits. For years, the local constable had turned a blind eye on nights when Angus drove home rolling drunk in the estate's battered old Landrover but finally the complaints from concerned villagers had forced him to act. Now, Angus had no driving licence and, as often as not, fell asleep in a ditch long before he reached the sparse comforts of the dilapidated bothy which he called home.

Alastair, on the other hand, was a gentle enthusiast, honest as the day is long, with a love of the country and 'his' lochs which bubbled over in his conversation and infectious chuckle. He was a fly tier of great skill and dexterity, and spent many a long evening peering at the vice on his little workbench over the rim of his spectacles. When, occasionally, he took it upon himself to visit the bar for some quiet conversation, much to the wicked delight of Angus and his cronies, his favourite tipple was an orange and soda.

For Alastair, the gem in his lord and master's fishing crown was a rich little loch which he and the estate workers had dammed many years ago and had since nurtured with loving care. The loch was, without doubt, the finest trout fishery for miles around. On a warm spring evening with the sedge emerging to skitter bank-wards across the still surface, there was no better place to be. Here the angler could experience the ultimate thrill: big brown trout feeding greedily on the surface, taking the artificial with confidence in the fading light. Alastair was justifiably proud and positively bubbled over with enthusiasm at the very thought of the loch.

Angus, of course, was jealous. He would not admit it to his cronies in the bar; indeed, he would barely admit as much to himself. But the jealousy was there nevertheless, like acid eating away at his sense of justice.

So, when Angus' son-in-law, visiting from the South to do a spot of coarse fishing on the 'big loch', came home one evening with a huge and evil-looking pike, Angus saw his chance to make mischief. A spirit of co-operation had always existed between the two estates; often one ghillie would negotiate a day's fishing on the neighbouring estate if things were slack. So when Angus arranged for his son-in-law to spend a day on Alastair's favourite little loch, Alastair suspected nothing out of the ordinary.

It was Alastair's wont, when he was not busy ghillie-ing on the river, to meet his client by the lochside at the end of the day, not principally in the expectation of a tip but more from a genuine desire to see how he had fared. So when Angus' son-in-law stepped from the boat, fingers hooked casually through the gills of a monster pike, an innocent smile lighting his face, Alastair was taken completely off guard. As the enormous implications of this calamitous discovery dawned on him, the colour alternately rose and then drained completely from the old man's face, leaving him pale and vulnerable looking, shoulders slumped, visibly shaken.

That night, Alastair's fly bench was, for once, untouched. He went to bed early; he did not have the energy to face the inquisition and ribaldry that was sure to await him in the pub. But before he retired, Alastair mustered sufficient energy to make a phone call to an old friend who worked in the fisheries laboratory down South. Stung by Alastair's obvious despair, his friend agreed to send one of his team the very next day to take samples from the loch and to look at the incriminating evidence.

The days passed and Alastair withdrew further and further into his own little world. He did not go out unless he had to; he did not speak unless spoken to; the ready smile had vanished. And then, one morning, a letter arrived in an envelope bearing the official Government stamp of the fisheries lab. Alastair did not open it right away. All through breakfast, he pointedly ignored the envelope staring down at him from the mantelpiece. Then, finally, with a shrug and a sigh of resignation, he fetched it down, slitting it open carefully and deliberately.

'So, in conclusion', the letter read, 'the evidence is indisputable; based on the scale readings and growth rate calculations, this fish cannot possibly have come from your loch.'

Alastair read that sentence twice. Second time around, the colour began to return to his cheeks and his shoulders gradually straightened. Poring over his vice that evening, the truth began to dawn.

It was months later; winter had drawn in, the bar was busy, laughter and rowdy banter rose and fell, smoke swirled thickly and condensation ran down the frosted window panes. Angus was sitting in his usual corner, hunched in deep conspiratorial conversation with several hard-drinking accomplices.

As Alastair walked in, blinking owl-like behind his spectacles as he adjusted to the dim light, Angus looked up and called a vulgar greeting across the room. Alastair smiled pleasantly back.

Half an hour later, the door opened again, this time admitting in a gust of cold air, the local constable and a serious-faced young man in a smart suit carrying a shiny document case. The constable strode purposefully over to the bar and tapped loudly on the counter, calling for silence. As the noise subsided, all eyes turned towards the intruders. Alastair sat quietly, unnoticed, the ghost of a smile playing on his lips.

The official looking gentleman cleared his throat and began in an authoritative voice:

'It has come to my attention that a crime has been committed under the terms of the Wildlife and Countryside Act 1981. It is a serious criminal offence to introduce new species to a body of water without a Government licence.'

The constable looked pointedly in Angus' direction, jangling the handcuffs hanging conspicuously at his belt. The grin vanished in a trice from Angus' face, his whisky glass froze half way to his lips and trembled visibly in shaking hands.

'Mr MacLeod', the constable intervened, 'are you able to save us a lot of trouble and identify the culprit here and now, so that I can take him into custody?'

Alastair played his part to perfection: 'Well, now', said he stroking his chin theatrically and dragging out the moment for maximum effect, 'let me see …'

From across the room, Angus tried hard to catch Alastair's eye, a pleading look of supplication on his face.

Alastair held the moment a little longer. Then, in a firm voice, clear in the hush that had descended about the bar, he spoke:

'I think we would all agree that the act in question was truly despicable.'

Out of the corner of his eye, Alastair saw Angus nod vigorously.

'Unfortunately,' Alastair continued, 'I can't say with complete certainty who was responsible … '

With a sigh, Angus sagged back into his seat, heedless of the spilled whisky dripping from the table into his lap. Grimly satisfied, Alastair felt as if a weight had finally been lifted from his shoulders. His precious loch was fine and he knew it would not be threatened again. He also knew that it would be some time before Angus dared to make fun of his old rival again.

All in all, he felt he deserved another orange and soda.

5

PLAYING WITH NUMBERS

I have kept a personal record of my fishing outings almost from the start. Though the first ten years or so were lost forever during one house move or another, the remaining twenty-six are all there. A bit like Muriel Foster's little diary published under the title *Days on Sea, Loch and River*, these journals record the 'where', the 'when', the 'hows' and the 'whys'. Occasionally, when the mood has taken, I have illustrated the pages with pen-and-ink sketches, recording for posterity my lasting impressions of the day.

When I look at these records with the benefit of hindsight, I can see subtle changes in emphasis over the years. In the early days, 'how big' and 'how many' featured large. Weights were recorded religiously for every fish. As time went by, the emphasis shifted towards the 'how', with copious and often detailed notes on flies, depths and retrieves. More recently still, the stark facts have given ground to the more prosaic. Anecdotes about people and places, descriptions of sights: things that will last longer in the memory than inches or ounces.

These journals have been, for me, an end rather than the means. Despite the wealth of statistics in their pages I have made no effort to explore or explain, never mind learn. But today, I intend to put that right.

Now, before I go any further, I should point out that the 'A' grade I received in SCE Higher Maths said more about my teacher than it did about myself. My performance in Statistics as an undergraduate (dismal) was a much more accurate reflection of my numeracy. So I have no intention of trying anything complex: no Chi squared, no T test, no normal distributions and positively no exponential curves. Just a couple of simple, straightforward plots.

The first one shows the number of fish I have caught per rod-day over more than a quarter of a century. What does this tell you? As so often with statistics, it seems, not much. Granted, you can see from the graph opposite when my fishing was restricted largely to the rainbow fisheries of the south where the fish are less accommodating and more wordly wise, just as you can pinpoint the years when I was able to return for a few days to the hills to boost my average. But, basically, it tells you nothing you could not already guess: fishing can be a lottery and I have learnt less over the years than I might have hoped.

The second graph, however, deserves closer scrutiny. The statistics are perhaps a little less sound, seeing as I have not always kept an entirely accurate record of fish risen and fish lost. For all that, it is undoubtedly a fair indication of my performance in this department.

You might expect to find the finely honed reactions of youth waning somewhat over the years. But not a bit of it. It needs no significance test to confirm the downward trend in the number of fish risen per fish caught (my 'conversion rate' as the serious angling writers like to call it). Could it be that experience is winning out after all, that the reactions have sharpened and the concentration improved with the passing years?

Perhaps, except that if you think a bit more deeply about it, there is a sting in the tail. If you accept that I am still catching pretty much the same number of fish I have always caught but rising fewer per fish caught, then it stands to reason that I am rising steadily fewer fish in total. So, do I congratulate myself on improving my conversion rate or bemoan the fact that my methods are deceiving progressively fewer and fewer fish?

Of course that, at the end of the day, is the trouble with statistical analysis. It shows you the trends but it does not help you explain them. It can cause a lot of tail-chasing and much soul searching, with remarkably little tangible benefit. I could be rising fewer fish because I am fishing less well. Or because I am fishing more difficult waters. Or simply, because I am losing my touch.

If pushed for an explanation, I would probably lean towards the view that all of this actually says more about the techniques I use than about my inherent ability to use them successfully. In common, I suspect, with most anglers, I have become much more comfortable with certain techniques over the years: principally, the techniques that I enjoy most. As the importance of catch diminishes, so I have gravitated increasingly towards these favoured techniques with less regard for the prevailing conditions.

It does not take Einstein (was he an angler?) to surmise that a size 14 Hawthorn Fly fished on the surface in a force 9 gale and sub-zero temperatures on the local stock-pond, probably results in less frequent displays of fishy interest than, say, a size 8 long-shank Viva in tandem with a fast sink line.

Why it should take forty years of fishing to realise that enjoyment of the

Catch Record

Conversion Rate

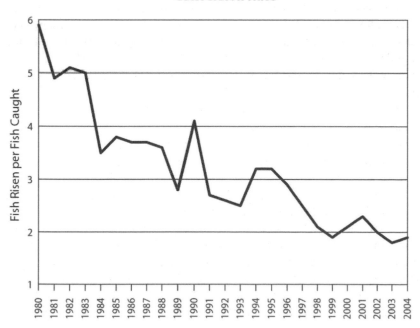

sport ultimately depends more on the way you fish than what you catch, is an interesting question in its own right. In retrospect, I suspect I actually came to this conclusion, subconsciously at least, a long time ago. It has just taken me a while to admit to it. The excitement when a fish comes to the surface or near-surface fly (be it wet or dry) and the heart-thumping moment when it takes, are feelings completely unparalleled in fishing.

Of course, I succumb to bouts of frustration when everyone around me is catching and I am not. And yes, I have been known to resort to less familiar approaches in times of desperation. I have even consulted books and videos in an ill-advised effort to broaden my horizons and find an answer for every twist and turn in the fishing day. But, when all is said and done, I know my preferences now and have accepted (more or less) that there will always be days when the trout get the better of me.

And that might be the end of this rather introspective analysis save for the twinge of conscience that compels me to make a disturbing admission. Until I do so, I fear I will be unable to rest in peace and continue keeping my records absolved of these nagging feelings of guilt.

You see, just occasionally, my rod average has been boosted (ever so slightly) by the retention of the odd trout over and above the official bag limit. Now, I know this is a dreadful offence and that there is no excuse adequate to explain my actions. I can only point out that, given current permit prices and my normal catch rate, most of the trout I take home are costly trout indeed. On the very odd occasion when my limited ability and range of techniques has allowed me the privilege of greater than normal success, I have no desire either to return my catch or to stop fishing and surrender part of my precious day out. On such occasions, I reckon the fishery manager owes me one or two.

I can already hear the chorus of voices proclaiming this to be a truly Scottish philosophy. And perhaps it is. But, in reality, it is a moral dilemma I never had to contend with in my formative years. In the hills, there is seldom a permit, never mind a bag limit. The major factor constraining the quality of the stock in the more remote hill lochs is, as often as not, the very abundance of fish. By taking my catch home, it could be argued that I am actually improving the quality of the fishing for those that follow.

There, I feel better now.

PART IX

LESSONS LEARNT

It is not the prettiest part of the world, Warrington; in fact I have heard it cruelly, and perhaps just a little unjustly, described as the 'armpit of England'. Neither does it aspire to any great cultural heights. Life revolves around lager, take-away food and 'the league' (Wilderspool on a sunny Saturday afternoon). But for all that, the people are amongst the friendliest I have come across. An otherwise miserable few months spent living out of one room in a Leigh guest house and dining on kebabs or fish and chips (sounds wonderful until the fifth or sixth consecutive evening, when even the most hardened cholesterol guzzler would kill for a salad or some nice crisp broccoli) was endured largely thanks to the welcoming openness of the people we met.

But inevitably, such gregarious spirit has its darker side: the average Warringtonite, male and female both, is a drinker par excellence. Despite the best university training, I soon recognised that I was out of my depth and gave up any pretence of equality. The evening which finally convinced me came at the end of my first squash season: the annual prize giving and boys' night out. Suspecting what was to come, I had prepared my ground well. I would leave in time for the last train home, 11.20 p.m., when things had barely livened up. And by some miracle, I did manage to find my way to the station on time. The choice, once there, was simple. There were but two trains at that hour: one went to Manchester (the right one) and the other went to Liverpool (the wrong one). I was half way to Liverpool before I realised that all was not as it should be.

1

WHEN WINNING
IS MORE IMPORTANT
THAN TAKING PART

I can honestly say that competition has rarely played a part in my fishing life. As Roderick Haig-Brown was quick to observe, angling is not a competitive sport and the angler's only real competition is with his quarry. The challenge is almost exclusively a personal one. Yet just occasionally, as if to shatter any cosy feelings of aloofness, the blood rises, the adrenaline flows and the friendly spirit of companionship suddenly develops a sharper edge. Invariably, it is a state of affairs that creeps up all unsuspected; by the time you recognise the symptoms for what they are, the feeling has taken hold and it is too late.

I well remember the triumphant expression on my friend's face when I returned from the hill lochs to find that he and the ghillie had taken three salmon from the Halladale on a hot, sunny day: a day on which I had been convinced that the trout were a much likelier bet. Or the guilty feeling of glee as I caught fish after fish the following season on little Loch Leir while my friend, from the same boat, could do nothing right. The final tally that day was eleven to three in my favour with the trusty little March Brown Spider doing most of the damage. Not as good as a salmon but at least honours were a little closer to even.

More recently, I experienced that same feeling closer to home, once again when I least expected it. By now, I considered myself, perhaps a touch pompously, to be a more mature fisher, cleansed of such juvenile and primitive urges. But then fishing, as I have alluded to before, has a nasty habit of surprising the unwary and shocking the self-righteous.

Carsington Reservoir, in the hills above Derby, was the venue. It was Carsington's first season and I had read about the rich feeding on newly flooded pastures and the rapidly growing trout gaining weight all through the unusually mild winter. My companions were the lads from the squash club, lads for whom competition was the spice of life, whether it be on squash court or in bar, so in truth I should have seen it coming. Before even we reached the water, liquid bets had been laid. And with these lads, I knew to my cost, the loser would pay dearly.

Yet despite my self-righteous indignation, the thicker the jibes flew, the faster my heart beat. By the time Carsington hove into view, a rare

atmosphere of pent-up excitement had mounted inside the car. Our first view of the reservoir, however, was something of a disappointment: a big, sprawling concrete car park and a non-descript water sports centre looking more than anything like some heartless motorway service station. Massed ranks of windsurfers plied the waters, knifing confidently through the waves or limping from one cold and painful reverse to the next.

But the beauty of Carsington lay in its size and the careful management of its resources, making it possible for the angler to escape the madding crowd and find his own solitude in the myriad of pretty little bays that cut deep into the fringe of pasture and woodland. Windsurfers, canoes and yachts were restricted to the open water around the dam, testimony to the exemplary care Severn Trent Water had taken to cater sensitively to the demands of potentially conflicting interests.

By the time we had purchased permits and unloaded the car, our little group was taut with purpose and happy determination. My companion and I stole a narrow lead as the two boats vied to see who would leave the jetty first. Our superior oarsmanship became evident as we pulled further away on the long row up the reservoir. Redgrave and Pinsent beware, we had the makings of an impressive team!

As we rowed, so the anticipation mounted. It was a touch on the cold side perhaps but there was a nice ripple on the surface and that encouraging light – not too bright but not too dull – which you get when the sun is hidden behind a thin layer of cumulus cloud. Although there was neither sight nor sound of splashing trout to lighten our toil, an indefatigable sense of optimism had us very much in its thrall.

I kicked off using my floating line as always, albeit less in expectation than on the premise that one fish caught on the surface is more satisfying than several caught deep, a personal foible developed over the years. Today, however, I secretly resolved not to dally. I meant business. If there were no signs of surface activity, I would not hesitate to resort to less esoterically satisfying techniques!

But such thoughts were quickly put on hold. As if responding to our mood of radiant optimism, a bright, lively brownie grabbed the little muddler minnow in scant inches of water, right where the ripples lapped up onto the newly flooded meadow.

Almost before the fish was netted, I noticed the opposition sidle closer, pushing the boundaries of good manners to the limit. They need not have bothered; this early success was to be a solitary one. Lunch came and went, and the peaceful face of the reservoir remained unsullied by further activity, leastways where we were fishing. By this time, the casting had degenerated, becoming noticeably frayed around the edges. Patience was on the wane.

Time, I decided, to sacrifice my principles! On went the 'deep sinker' and a team of nymphs, leaded pheasant tail on the point to get the cast down. We found a quiet spot over about fifteen feet of water, anchored and began a systematic exploration of the depths. The opposition had drifted out of sight now, no doubt reckoning that we were no better able to unlock the reservoir's mysteries than they. As the first couple of casts inched back to the surface unhindered, I began to think they might be right.

On the third cast, I forced myself to count down from one hundred before starting the retrieve. Either we had made a major miscalculation, or my flies must be hard on the bottom by now. I began a slow figure of eight retrieve. This time, almost before the first coils hit the bottom of the boat, I felt the satisfying drag as a fish intercepted the little Hare's Ear plying its wares on the middle dropper.

Less than an hour later, my six fish bag limit was complete: two more to the Hare's Ear and two to a tiny Black Buzzer. A finer bag of fish you could not wish to see: brown trout in the peak of condition, full finned, plump and cheerfully spotted in red and black. My feelings of pride were heightened by the sure knowledge that I had won; already we had watched the opposition slink wearily back towards the jetty. I could almost feel the envy and taste the Theakston's already!

How, I mused contentedly as we rowed back through the gathering gloom, should I play it? Overbearing modesty, I decided, was most appropriate to the occasion.

And when we finally reached the jetty, there was a wonderful bonus to come. The opposition had not merely been less successful, they had, in fact, failed altogether! Being a responsible angler, I weighed and recorded my catch outside the fishing hut where my companions were gathered, taking great pain to remove the fish from the bass one by one (in the interests of an accurate return, of course).

A little later, winding down in the cosy cheerfulness of the local hostelry, I reflected smugly that the Theakston's tasted better than usual that night. The company, perhaps, was a little muted …

That day on Carsington, a relationship began which was to strengthen over the next couple of seasons. For the first time, I had found something resembling a 'home water'. Granted, it was ninety minutes away by car on a good day but it was an attractive venue, with good fishing, enough variety to hold a few secrets in reserve and, best of all, exclusively a brown trout water.

For the first time in many years, I was experiencing the pleasures of familiarity: getting to know a fishery in all its moods; experimenting with different flies and different techniques; occasionally feeling the satisfaction of catching fish on a difficult day.

I knew the corner where, with the wind in the right quarter, little black hawthorn flies drifted onto the water to be sucked delicately beneath the surface film, as martins swooped and dived ecstatically above. Then, the only likely tactic was a tiny, black, dry fly, and even finely-tuned reactions and razor-sharp eyesight did not always guarantee success.

As the autumn approached and the first golden leaves danced on the breeze to drift lazily across the water's surface, I witnessed the thrilling sight of big brown trout slashing mercilessly through shoals of fry in water so shallow that shiny backs glinted in the sun, dorsal fins standing proudly erect.

I even knew where to look for that rarity, the evening rise, and occasionally caught trout under the overhanging trees as leather-winged bats flitted on silent wings and the gathering gloom distorted distances, turning bank-side bushes into strange and frightening shapes.

Such are the intimate pleasures and thrills that familiarity can bring and that Carsington unveiled for me. They were experienced alone, however. The squash lads have not been back.

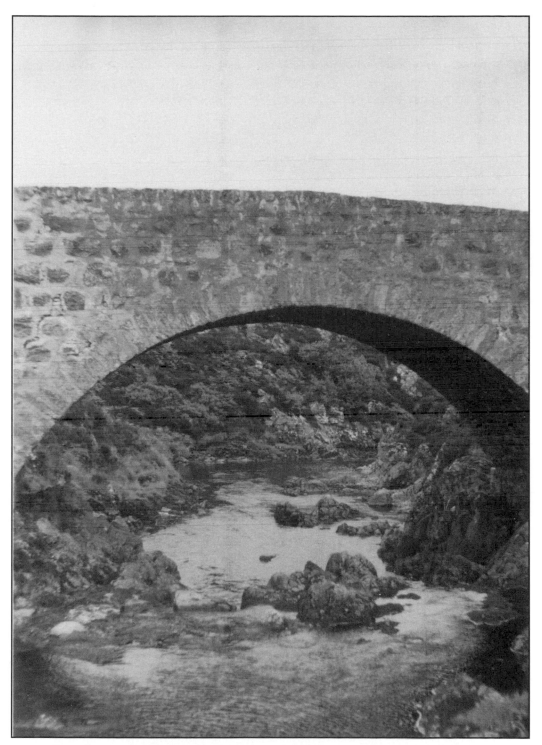

Low flow on the Halladale, Caithness: time to concentrate on the hill lochs

2

SKELETONS
IN THE FLY BOX

I wonder if we all have that compartment in our fly box, the 'graveyard compartment', the compartment full of flies ineptly tied in moments of mad inventiveness, gaudy monstrosities which would not look out of place hanging from the rafters on Christmas Eve: flies which have only one thing in common − they have never caught a fish and in the cold light of day are never likely to.

And yet every time space is short and I begin to consider a bit of a clear out, a little voice somewhere tells me to leave well alone. And so the compartment is shut, not to be opened again until next time lack of space for the more conventional occupants produces a twinge of conscience.

But that's not quite the whole story. Sometimes, just once in a while, along comes that day when the wind is in the wrong quarter, the sun is too strong, the fish are down and nothing seems to work. Suddenly, quite without warning, the fingers start to twitch and almost before you know it, there they are, those long neglected creations staring plaintively up from your lap. With a furtive glance to make sure the bailiff is not watching, some malformed monstrosity is extricated, tied quickly onto the cast (by now shortened from many despairing changes), cast out more in hope than expectation, retrieved uninterrupted, and immediately consigned whence it came with a shrug and a mental 'I told you so'.

So this is a story dedicated to those malformed occupants of the graveyard compartment, a story which will perhaps provide a ray of hope in their otherwise wretched existence.

Sometime before, when a business colleague had invited me to join him for an afternoon's fishing on a little private fishery just a stone's throw from the M6 motorway, a fishery which he assured me was stocked with very obliging rainbows, I did not take long to consider my answer.

Now, somewhere along the line, I think my colleague had formed the idea that, whilst perhaps enthusiastic, I was a little wet behind the ears when it came to the gentle art. Being a canny Scot and well versed in the vagaries of fishing, I was not about to disabuse my friend of his theory. I certainly did not let on that I had been fishing pretty much since I learned to walk.

The appointed day arrived and not even sun shining from a brassy sky and water the consistency of green porridge could dampen my spirits. Thoughts of drifting and floating lines were quickly dispelled, and at my companion's suggestion, we resorted to a style with which I have never been very comfortable. We anchored up and began painstakingly to explore the depths.

To cut a long and very frustrating story short, we tried everything. Damsel nymphs inched along the bottom, carefully presented buzzers, big lures stripped back towards the boat like nothing ever witnessed in nature. Many well-deserved reputations for infallibility were shattered that afternoon. I began to doubt whether anything actually lived beneath the deceptively welcoming surface of that little lake.

And then suddenly, without a conscious thought and without, it seemed, moving a muscle, the graveyard compartment lay open on my lap, its occupants glaring malevolently up at me like so many refugees from the twilight zone. Like magnets, my eyes were drawn irrevocably towards the vilest of all the graveyard's occupants. It had been spawned one particularly dark and forbidding night the previous winter. Distraught, like Baron Frankenstein, at the enormity of my creation, I could not even bring myself to perform a proper christening. And yet like the Baron too, some vague paternal instinct had prevented me from taking the merciful course of action. Instead, that nameless horror had been consigned to its miserable existence alongside the graveyard's other sad failures. Until, that was, this fateful July day.

The beads adorning the shank of the hook made a splash that sent a family of coots scurrying for cover as the nameless thing hit the surface some distance from the boat. My host looked round in horror, no doubt on the verge of making some comment about my artless casting. I did not need to recite the national anthem while waiting for this one to sink; it plunged to the bottom like a torpedo pursuing a submarine.

Slowly I began my retrieve. By the time the offspring of my invention was halfway back towards the boat I had already decided, in my shame, to return it whence it came. When, a few long, slow draws later, the line stopped with that dead feeling indicative of heavy, clinging weed, I breathed a sigh of relief. It looked as though my creation would receive merciful freedom at last.

And then a strange thing happened. The 'weed' began to move, slowly at first, then with gathering pace. Panic stricken, I fumbled to retrieve the lengths of loose line at my feet as my no doubt baffled quarry made its desperate bid for freedom. As it happened, I need not have worried; that fish was stuck tighter than a cork in a bottle.

Seconds later, as I looked down at the shining flank and full fins of a cock rainbow in his prime, my mind felt numb. Surely this had to be a fluke. After all, everyone knows that one swallow does not make a spring. And yet some deep-seated instinct persuaded me to grant my protégé a brief stay of execution. So, with my friend's fulsome praise and congratulations still ringing in my ears, my line snaked out again with renewed vigour.

This time, the coots were ready and dove scant moments before the object of their terror hit the surface. Once more the slow retrieve, once more the rising doubt, once more the lethargic resistance followed almost immediately by the satisfying thump of a well-hooked fish deep beneath the surface. This time I swear my colleague's praise was tinged with a faint note of envy. After all, my monster had no companion.

When, moments later, the same sequence of events was repeated for a third time, his concern was palpable and my modesty, shamefully false.

Late into that night, when more respectable anglers were safely tucked up in bed dreaming of tomorrow's fish, a lone figure worked feverishly in his fly-tying laboratory, desperately trying to clone his monstrous creation. Thoughts of patents and untold wealth lent urgency to trembling fingers. Yet try as he might, the magic had gone.

Many times since have I plied close likenesses in identical conditions, on similar waters, only to see my creations rejected with a depressing finality. Never again, it seems, can I recreate the true essence of my original Frankenstein. Yet still the memory of that day lingers. What, I wonder, made those fish fall for a fly with no passing resemblance to anything of nature born? Could it have been, quite simply, a craving for the taste of something different, the piscine equivalent of adventurous living?

Whatever the answer, next time you have one of these impossible days, take hope, for in that forgotten compartment of your fly box may lurk your own Frankenstein. Such is the mystery and fascination of fishing.

Time to leave before the midges descend

3

THE ONE THAT GOT AWAY

No fishing book would be complete without the tale of what might have been; this one is no different. My wife and I were spending a few days at the Shieldaig Lodge Hotel on the north west coast of Scotland not far from the little fishing village of Gairloch. We planned to finish our brief stay fishing the Fairy Lochs, a group of small lochs a short walk into the hills from the hotel, whose strange and descriptive names – Top Fairy, Spectacles, Diamond and Aeroplane – were things to conjure with and had long fascinated us.

The first of these, Top Fairy, was renowned as a dour loch but a loch which contained good fish. Looking back through the hotel's records in the bar the night before, it was clear that the reputation was well deserved. Top Fairy, despite being fished regularly, rarely seemed to produce more than one or two fish per season but we had to look hard to find a fish from the loch less than two and a half pounds in weight.

Today, the weather was mild but a strong and blustery wind blew from the south-west making casting a difficult and occasionally, a hazardous occupation. We started with a few casts on Top Fairy and, true to form, saw not fin, nor scale, of a fish.

Walking on over the hills we came next to Aeroplane. As we climbed down to the banks we were surprised to find that the loch appeared round in shape; certainly it bore no resemblance that we could see to an aeroplane. The wind dropped as we descended until, by the time we reached the spongy, sphagnum shoreline, the air was almost preternaturally still. The loch itself was dominated by an island with a strangely warped and stunted tree sprouting in its midst. As I walked round the bank, intent on scanning the surface for activity, I tripped on a solid object in my path. Looking down, I saw a ragged metal sheet protruding from the heather with printing barely

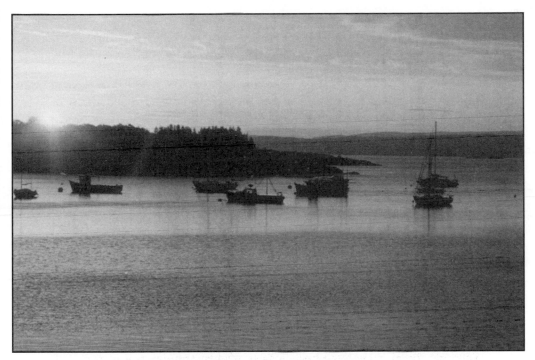

Shieldaig Bay on a rare still evening

legible on its corroded and pitted surface.

With mounting horror, the pieces began to fit together in my head. I looked up and my eyes settled on the island. My heart missed a beat. That was no tree, it was the twisted wreckage of a warplane, most probably an American bomber disoriented by the drifting mists and lured to a watery grave. As I walked on around the bank, I came across more and more evidence from the loch's melancholy past, much of it preserved in eerily pristine condition as if in defiance of the elements.

Halfway round the loch, I met up with my wife. She too had cast hardly a line, she too had felt the disconcerting stillness of the place and had reached the same grisly conclusions. We agreed wordlessly to leave the loch and her past to slumber undisturbed. As we clambered back up the slope in silence, the wind rose again and stayed with us for the rest of the day.

We fished the long and narrow Diamond Loch next, catching only a few tiny fish before moving on to the dark little Spectacles, two lochs interconnected by a narrow channel to give them their name. Even in the fishy shelter of the Spectacles' high banks under the overhanging rowan trees, nothing moved. Somehow, it seemed, the mood of the day had been set.

By now, the wind was strengthening and rain clouds were gathering ominously dark on the horizon. Already, the roaring fire and the cosy little bar of the old Victorian hotel seemed to beckon with a growing allure. What better place from which to view the rain sweeping into Shieldaig Bay and watch the little boats bob in agitation at their moorings.

Minds made up, we started the climb back to meet the track at the end of Top Fairy. Long before we got there, the heavens opened and sheets of rain swept remorselessly across the unfriendly landscape to find unexpected ways inside our heavy-duty waterproofs.

By the time Top Fairy finally came into view, we were soaked beyond redemption. Burns were running where, scant hours before, the ground had been dry and crisp. Amongst the sphagnum beds, butterwarts and sundew opened their glistening leaves in anticipation. Water dripped from bog cotton, as though from the end of an old man's beard. I should have been miserable but perversely, as long as I knew a hot bath awaited at the other end, I was content. I had that feeling of exultation, childlike in its simplicity, which adults are not supposed to feel on a day such as this.

So when we reached Top Fairy, rather than continue immediately on down the path, I decided to stop for just a few casts from that enticing looking spit of land at the end of the loch. As I fished round the point I remembered afresh Top Fairy's reputation. Who was I to expect to catch a fish here on my first attempt when others had tried for season after season without success?

Looking back up the loch to where my wife huddled miserably in the shelter of the cliff face, too cold to fish, I determined to make the next cast my last. Out snaked the line across the foam-streaked surface. On the first gentle pull, there was an unexpected swirl and I felt a light resistance. So light that, instead of tightening immediately as I would normally have done, I raised the rod tip in somewhat desultory fashion almost as an afterthought, thinking that it was just my luck to hook the only undersize trout in the loch. No sooner had the thought formed in my mind than, as if by way of retort, the object attached to the end of my cast took off with all the awesome power of a nuclear submarine.

Shocked belatedly into more positive action, I took control as best I could. No permanent damage, it seemed, had been done. The battle raged on, first one protagonist on top, then the other. As the minutes dragged by, I still had not seen my opponent. Then, all of a sudden, the nature of the battle changed. In a fit of pique, perhaps at the audacity of this intrusion on its liberty, my quarry hurled itself from the water in a dazzling display of tail-stands, more in the flamboyant fashion of some deep-sea game fish than a trout in a little Scottish hill loch.

The sight brought my heart leaping into my mouth; surely here, at last, was my first three-pound trout! And the battle was turning my way.

Excitedly, I unclipped the net and slid it carefully into the water at my feet in readiness. My quarry was on his side now, his heavy, spotted head sliding across the very rim of the net. In that moment, a glassy eye fixed me with a balefully defiant glare and from somewhere he found the strength to kick one last time. That was all it took, fly and fish parted company, and my record trout slid quietly back beneath the surface to fight another day. Not for nothing the reputation of the Top Fairy trout.

For a long moment I could only stand there, cast fluttering in the wind, disbelief and anguish etched together on my face. Then I swore once, loudly, and headed back towards the base of the cliff. Although my wife had watched the battle excitedly and later bore witness to my quarry's prodigious leaps, she had no comfort to offer. What could she say to take away my despair?

Suddenly, I was aware of the rain seeping through the seat of my trousers and coursing in rivulets down my neck. All I wanted was to reach the comfort of the hotel and to drown my sorrows.

No, all I really wanted was to have these few moments again. But that, I knew, was not to be.

Postscript

On 12 July 2004, lightening struck for a second time.

It was a pleasant day and I had a plump 1 ½ lb. brownie in the creel from 'Rabbit Warren Run'. I was fishing down a nice pool below the suspension bridge when my little weighted shrimp stopped dead. I tightened, suspecting only that I had hit the bottom. I had caught some nice fish on the Wharfe over the years but nothing that could be described as a monster. Natural recruitment is augmented by an annual stocking programme but the fish are expected to earn their spurs in the wild and are not stocked at exceptional sizes.

The weight at the end of my line began moving, at gathering speed, down the pool. In the moments that followed, I could do little else but hang on. Just when it looked as if my unseen protagonist was about to disappear forever into the pool below, there was a wild thrashing on the surface and the line went momentarily slack as the fish did a U-turn and steamed back up the pool towards me. I hauled the line in frantically and just about managed to keep in touch.

One more run across the pool, the roll of a heavy body on the surface and I had the net unclipped in anticipation. Perhaps my mistake was daring to believe that here, surely, was my first wild 3 lb. brown trout. At that precise moment, the line went slack with that sickening finality that could mean but one thing ... all these years on, I am still waiting.

4

SURPRISE PACKAGES

In different circumstances, I might have scratched my head and declared sagely that one of the attractions of fishing is the element of surprise: you can never tell what the weather is going to do, never mind when (or if) you are going to encounter the fish of a lifetime.

Yet predictability can be re-assuring and I have recently been moved more than once to think that a bit of certainty in fishing, not to mention the wider parish of life, might not be such a bad thing. This thought, if indeed I was still capable of thinking rationally at all, was at the forefront of my mind as I trudged back to the holiday chalet in the half light, water seeping through the lining of my coat, legs aching, knees creaking.

In truth, I should have seen it coming. But despite the evidence of my own eyes and the gloomy tones of the weatherman on the car radio, I had continued to cling stubbornly to the hope that things might improve.

We were on Skye for just a few days and the evening pass had been hard-earned. By the time I had thrown some tackle together and driven out along the cliff top to the end of the winding single-track road, the sky had darkened and the drizzle was sweeping in from the sea with that peculiar single-mindedness typical of the West Highlands. In truth, it looked as if the sun might never shine again. Yet my mood remained positive. I had identified a chain of three lochs on the map, none of which I had fished before. That element of the unknown, together with an energising feeling of freedom, had got the adrenaline pumping. Even the icy blast that hit me full in the face as I opened the car door and peered with watering eyes into the rapidly descending gloom, could not suppress my optimism entirely.

The first part of the hike was easy. The rocky track threaded its way confidently across the landscape. On another day, judging where to strike out and follow the burn into the hills would not have been difficult. In the event, two days of intermittent rainfall had turned much of the hillside into a streaming torrent of water, every gully looking alike as it rumbled and foamed with dark, peat-stained water.

In the end, I took an educated guess and started the long scramble up the hillside, through knee high heather, heavy with water. The gully ahead looked promising, about the right size to hold a lochan. But, as each new horizon came and went, I saw only more heather, more outcrops of lichen-covered rock, slick with water, more sheets of drizzle driving across the barren landscape.

Eventually, lungs close to bursting, I sat down in the heather to get my breath back. All around, immense spiders' webs bowed under the weight of raindrops, while their occupants cowered deep in the vegetation, conserving their energy. A rabbit scurried along the sheep track unaware that, high above, a buzzard was soaring, struggling to hold its station on the wind, desperate to locate a meal for its hungry chicks on a day when little stirred.

For all that, a feeling of confidence endured. This was not the first time it had taken what seemed an age to locate a previously untried loch. Having recovered my breath, I clambered laboriously to the top of the nearest peak to get my bearings. But once again, the view that greeted my eager eyes was not re-assuring. Nothing but heather, bog and rock. No sign, ironically in a landscape dripping with water, of my goal. Perhaps I should cut my losses. But no, that stubborn little voice broke in; this was an opportunity not to be wasted.

Trusting to my instincts once more, I headed off in what I surmised to be a westerly direction. Two ridges came and went. Still nothing. It had not seemed so far on the map.

No sooner had my optimism finally begun to wane than I mounted the next ridge to see the first lochan stretching out ahead of me, shrouded in swirling mists, barely fifty yards from where I stood. As I waded through sphagnum heavy with water, the tiredness slipped magically away as it always did. The clinging dampness of my clothing seemed naught but a minor encumbrance.

But the extra couple of feet gained as I clambered onto solid ground and heaved my tackle bag off my shoulder changed my perspective completely. The water stretching before me was covered, bank to bank, with a thick mat of reeds and lily pads. I sighed in frustration but assembled my tackle anyway. This too had happened before. Usually, around one headland or another, it was possible to find at least a few square yards of open water. Often, the really big fish chose to patrol such spots.

But not tonight. There were, quite simply, no gaps in the vegetation big enough to take a cast. I scrambled around the length of the shore without casting a line. Oblivious to my presence, the occasional splash amongst the lily pads provided frustrating evidence that the loch held a good head of trout and only accentuated the hopelessness of my cause. My frame of mind deteriorated noticeably.

Trying to ignore the clinging dampness of my clothing, I heaved my bag onto my shoulder and started the trek up the little connecting burn towards the next loch. On the map, this one looked to be bigger. At least I should be able to wet a line. But this time my fate was apparent long before I reached the water's edge. From the top of the rise, I could hear the rushes sigh in the strengthening wind and see them bend and straighten in swathes like a green wave rippling from one shore to the other.

I grimaced inwardly and scowled at the leaden skies as I turned to trudge the length of the loch in search, once more, of the connecting burn and the passage onwards: not a difficult task, as the burn threatened to break its banks and make the narrow gully impassable. The climb seemed interminable this time. The wind funnelled down the gully, whistling through the heather, causing the bog cotton to bob like a flotilla of tiny ships at the mercy of a violent sea.

This time, there was no room for decorum. I swore out loud at the site that greeted my pinched eyes. More lilies, more reeds, more sphagnum bog. But wait, could that be a patch of open water right up at the very furthest end of the loch? As my vision cleared, I realised that it was, albeit not much bigger than the top of a kitchen table.

I stumbled on towards my goal, eyes focussed on that little piece of salvation. Edging along the none-too-stable looking peat bank, undercut by the erosive effects of the loch, I got myself into position and, at last, sent a tentative line snaking out across the surface.

Contemptuously, a gust of wind turned my cast aside and I watched helplessly as my flies landed amongst the lilies crowding in around the edges of the open water. I jerked my line off the surface in an ill-advised effort to thwart imminent disaster. Too late. All my action achieved was to embed the tail fly firmly in the fleshy stem of a lily pad. This time, I did not bother to hold back the string of choice words. The wind simply whisked my utterances away mockingly, erasing all trace of my feelings.

It took ten minutes for stiff, cold fingers to change the cast and tie on a new team of wet flies. The wind made my eyes water so that I could barely see the knots I was tying and droplets of water ran down the bridge of my nose to splash into my open fly wallet. I could only grit my teeth and get the job done, wasting as little time as possible.

With the benefit of hindsight, I made allowance for the wind and my flies landed where I had intended, right along the edge of the lily bed, just where you might expect a fish to be lying in wait. I retrieved, full of expectation: nothing. Two more casts: still nothing.

I was, finally, on the point of giving up. Charitable thoughts about the anticipation of discovery and the thrill of unpredictability were, it is fair to say, diminishing rapidly. One last cast and I was on my way. My flies landed squarely across the middle of the open water. It took just two pulls before an almighty explosion of water and foam engulfed the tail fly. Taken completely by surprise, I jumped, jerked the rod tip mightily and screamed in sheer frustration as a broken cast pinged back towards me to land in an untidy heap amongst the reeds, the one remaining fly embedding itself up to the shank.

I stood stock-still for a moment, ignoring the rain coursing down my neck, holding my bowed head in wet, cold hands, all the while cursing in language I barely knew I possessed. The wind hurled my curses scornfully back at me. Then I tugged the flies free, picked up my gear and started back, heedless of the broken cast flapping forlornly at the end of my rod.

If it is fair to say that I had set myself up for that miserable evening on Skye, I had perhaps more reason to feel aggrieved a season later, when a day's fishing on Sutton Bingham down in Somerset, failed to follow the script.

By way of contrast, this day was fine. I had shed all but the last layer of protective clothing and was well on my way to a fine tan. This was a brief break and I was returning soon to a new job: a job I had not asked for and a job I did not want. But today, the nagging worries were melting in the gentle heat of the sun and the peaceful stillness of my surroundings. My spirits were high. Let tomorrow look after itself.

Despite such positive feelings, a distant leap had hitherto provided the only tangible evidence of the rainbows I had been told inhabited the reservoir's sparkling waters and reedy margins. But not any more. For the past several minutes, I had been watching with mounting excitement, the repeated boil of a fish feeding over a shallow mud-bank just within casting distance. From where I stood, heron-like in the shallows, I could see plumes of mud drifting from the vicinity of the activity, confirming that something large was grubbing around for a meal.

Satisfied that it was not just the effects of imminent heat stroke, I put on a little weighted corixa and cast out across the mud-bank. The corixa landed with a satisfying plop and quickly sank out of sight. For once, my tactics worked like a charm; it took just two small twitches before the line tightened. I lifted the rod tip and the fish took off towards the horizon, the little fly firmly embedded in its scissors. I had never felt anything like it. This was a hefty specimen seemingly oblivious to any pressure I might apply. As I held on, the fish simply continued in its oddly unhurried, almost stately fashion.

After all these years of patient waiting, I thought, this was what a really big rainbow felt like. No splashing and fuss, just a good solid pull and the conviction that this was a truly worthy opponent. I could only continue to hold on and await developments.

It took several minutes and a lot of firm pressure before I finally managed to turn his head and retrieve a little line. I was still surprised by the tenor of the battle but I was in new territory here, so I was learning as I went along. If such dour and unspectacular tactics were typical of big trout, then so be it, I was prepared for that.

By the time the fish was circling slowly towards the extended landing net, my arms were sore with the strain. Yet still the fish had not revealed so much as a fin. As if determined to compound the mystery, a dense veil of mud, stirred by my shifting waders, concealed my coveted prize for a little longer.

It was only as I stretched forward and drew the fish firmly towards the rim of the net, convinced that a rainbow of five pounds or more was within my grasp, that my foe finally showed himself in all his glory. For a wonderful instant, my heart leapt at his sheer bulk. But as he keeled over on his side, exposing a deep copper flank patterned with heavy, armour-like scales, the truth finally hit me and the sun ceased to shine. For ten minutes, I had been doing battle with a leviathan. But not with the massive rainbow of my dreams.

I had just landed a specimen carp. I wished I hadn't.

PART X
NEW RESPONSIBILITIES

Thinking about starting a family was one thing. Starting one, I suspected, would be quite another.

And now that the die was cast and my wife was getting more cumbersome by the day, I was having doubts. The National Childbirth Trust was not helping much either. Sitting on the midwife's carefully manicured lawn, sipping tea, watching a bevy of rotund mothers-to-be enthusiastically 'give birth' to a battered old rag doll and listening to tales of 'how it really was', did little for my peace of mind.

The truth was simple. Either you are receptive to change or you are not, and deep down, I suspect, most of us are not. Giving up the freedom of a bachelor's life was a sacrifice that made me guard what was left of my individuality all the more stringently. How would I cope with work after a sleepless night? What would I do when my son (or daughter, for that matter) came home from school with a Warrington accent asking to be taken to Wilderspool on a Saturday afternoon? How could I endure the cataclysmic possibility of rearing a child who wore white when England played? And, worst of all, without grandparents near to share the burden, how would I ever escape to the waterside with rod, line and head full of tangled thoughts?

1

HOBSON'S CHOICE

It was a cold, stinging rain, a rain which drummed on the window of the fishing hut and filled the little boat faster than I could bail, the sort of rain that fish do not like.

Having a young family is an exercise in time management. That is why I was reduced to such a day and such a loch. Fishing alone on the occasional half-day fitted haphazardly between trips to the children's farm (whose inmates suffered endless indignities with an air of serene resignation which I had never quite mastered) and rainy day dashes across the yard to the little indoor swimming pool, I was left with whichever loch those higher on the rota did not want, usually Nam Fiodhag.

'It's fishing, Jim, but not as we know it … ' I reflected grimly as I sat in the hut watching the puddles grow around my feet, warming numb hands on the plastic coffee cup and listening distractedly as wave upon wave of rain lashed the exposed north-west side of the hut. Outside, a gull squawked in protest as it foolishly took to the wing and was instantly whipped away over the tops of the thrashing conifers. Only the spider, crouching motionless in the beams above, seemed unconcerned.

The water was already noticeably higher than when I had arrived, lapping amongst the heather roots and turning the area around the hut into a black, peaty quagmire. The only thing that kept me here was the sure knowledge that in seventy-two hours time I would be far south, sweating in an overheated office, dealing with one pointless panic after another and wishing I were here. But for all that, I could not face the indignity of sitting on a sodden boat seat once more, or the pain of bailing with an empty bean can and hands red raw from the last drift. And anyway, I had caught nothing and seen nothing.

Time for a last ditch change of tactics. Remembering the ghillie's suspiciously gushing comments about the wealth of feeding available around Nam Fiodhag's stony shores when I was allocated the loch for the third successive time, I put a little shrimp on the tail and with a deep breath, hoisted my fishing bag across one shoulder and stepped outside. Instantly, the door was ripped from my hands and crashed against the side of the hut, bucking and heaving like a maddened rodeo bronco.

Moments later, I was down on the shoreline where the banks proffered at least a modicum of shelter from the worst ravages of the elements. My first few casts were forced out across the wind, cutting through the water's surface like a sharp knife into butter. As I retrieved, dark gusts played across the roiling waters, skating my flies over the top. Nothing happened.

My wrist near breaking, I gave in and directed my next cast instead at right angles to the wind along the shoreline, in amongst the flooded heather roots. An instant later, the line tightened and a fish surged out of the shallows leaving a v-wake on the surface. He was game, well-hooked and over three-quarters of a pound, a shade bigger than anything I had taken from Nam Fiodhag before.

Neither was this to prove a fluke. As I squelched gently through the margins dropping the little shrimp amongst the tangled vegetation, I caught one fish after another: good, solid, plump hill loch trout. By six o'clock, I had a basket of nine. The action was engrossing and my thoughts did not stray in anger to cold fingers or wet feet until I sat once more in the shelter of the hut, pondering this unexpected turn of events and looking in admiration tinged with a little sadness at the torn, battered remnant of my game little point fly.

I returned two days later on the final day of the holiday. The conditions were much the same, though perhaps a touch milder, a shrimp of similar size and design on the point, and I was full of enthusiasm and confidence. All day I fished amongst the margins; it was the only day I returned empty-handed on that holiday.

I slunk home bewildered, exasperated and with a strong feeling that the older I got, the less I understood.

CHILD'S PLAY

Icould not quite dismiss the feeling that life had turned full cycle. Here I was watching my eldest son standing still for as long as I had ever seen, peering intently at the rain-pocked surface of the pond where a large yellow float bobbed defiantly.

True, it was a far cry from the wild, remote burns of my own childhood but the concentration and the serious expression on the boy's face were, I was certain, no different. Despite the intense effort apparent in the set of his shoulders, it was asking a lot of a three-year-old to focus the mind for long, and so far, each time the float had bobbed beneath the surface, the child's thoughts and gaze had been elsewhere. I was beginning to fear that my son's introduction to the gentle art might be a painful, if realistic, one.

The rain was heavier now and I could see he was getting restless. A large drip had formed on the end of his nose and the wild mop of strawberry blonde hair was plastered to his scalp like an exotic skullcap. The boy shifted uncomfortably and turned towards his father to utter, I was sure, a heartfelt complaint.

At that precise moment, in answer to my silent prayer, the float was drawn firmly beneath the surface once more. This time, I lunged forward to jerk the rod tip upwards, surprising the child so much that he lost his footing and sat down with a squelch and a cry on the bare, muddy bank. In the excitement and panic which ensued, the boy responded to his father's urgent exhortations and turned the handle on the reel ... the wrong way.

That fish must have been the unluckiest rainbow trout in all Christendom, for in complete defiance of logic he remained hooked while father and son sorted themselves out. Playing him now with two large and two small hands side by side on the rod butt, I prayed that no further misadventure would overtake us. A few seconds later, I swung the unfortunate fish ashore while Watson Minor quite literally danced up and down in excitement and released tension.

That fish was followed by another better one, perhaps a pound and a bit in weight. The fleeting thought crossed my mind that I had fished for years before catching a fish much more than half this size, and that my son's impression of the angling game might just be a touch jaundiced as a result. But that mattered not. This was his moment and the tramp back past the stew ponds to the little hut to collect his certificate was accompanied by ceaseless, excited chatter which bubbled forth in merriment, just like that little burn where my own fishing life had begun so many years before.

By the time we got to the car and related the tale to Grandpa, who was wakened with a visible start from a guiltily stolen snooze, the child had become a brave hero, fighting to the death with some great, mythical monster and bearing its body home in triumphant splendour.

Grandpa smiled quietly, dreamed a little and exchanged a knowing glance with me.

3

BETWEEN A ROCK
AND A HARD PLACE

s the gathering army of onlookers sidled closer, there was no sign that my silent prayers would be answered: the rock remained a rock. The thought fleetingly crossed my mind that I was past the age for childish deceptions. But now was not the time for philosophical debate and I instantly consigned that thought to the dusty file in the darkest recesses of my brain, marked 'pending'.

The day had started promisingly. I had caught a nice trout while all around me had failed, seemingly ensnared in the sleepy doldrums of a gentle summer afternoon. But, as is so often the case when fishing such waters, my early success had flattered to deceive. Not that I minded greatly, I had reached that happy state of Nirvanah that fishing sometimes bestows, lifting the mind to a higher plane where the act of casting is automatic and distant, and the angler fades into the background like the vague figure in an old watercolour, more shadow than substance. It is a soothing state of mind that I rarely tire of.

Close by, sun sparkled off flying droplets as a family of coot puddled comically in the shallows, ducking under the water, then surfacing to flap their stubby wings. One chick emerged with a head-dress of water weed not unlike those garish wigs so beloved of the modern day cricket follower. A dazzling dragonfly flitted in and out of the margins, manoeuvring with breathtaking dexterity, clearly intent on terrorising all that entered his domain. The occasional rainbow broke the surface but with the sort of theatrical leap seldom indicative of any serious dietary intent.

Such days were created for idle muse and quiet reflection. There was no place within them for the whirr of double hauls, the plop of giant lures and the shouted ribaldry that suddenly interrupted my reverie, and sent the dragonfly zipping up and across the bank to pursue his business elsewhere. Fishing on the local stock ponds, I had come to accept (to some degree at least) that it was not always possible to escape such intrusions and I had learned to shut my mind to everything beyond my immediate vicinity. This was not always easy, however, especially when the perpetrators achieved something I found very difficult: they caught fish.

Today, I was confident, would be no different. I had seen it all before: the back cast that caused the delicate ragged robin high on the bank behind to shiver in anticipation of a summary beheading; the forward cast lashing the water's surface, causing the reflections to dance and shatter into a million pieces; and finally, the thud of flies hitting the water like a series of cluster bombs. They hogged the best 'swims', they sullied nature's face with beer cans and noise. But worst of all, they caught fish.

Yes, I admit it, my loathing was tinged with more than a little self-righteous jealousy. No amount of delicate casting, no amount of experimentation ever seemed to avail me in the slightest. Time and again, I had been forced to suffer while my co-habitants hauled in fish after fish with monotonous regularity and brazen, shouted declarations of success.

And yet it was not the catching of fish itself that spoiled my mood: no, rather, it was not knowing how they did it. Curiosity ate away at me, consuming my thoughts when all I wanted to do was disengage from all form of cerebral activity. I knew that if I looked at the fishery log at the close of the day, I would find no answers. I knew that I did not have the humility to ask for advice and I knew with certainty, because I had tried it before, that any attempt to dawdle as I passed on the bank would tell me nothing worth knowing.

And that is why I had got myself into the fix I was in.

The rock continued to sulk as the opposition moved closer still, as yet unsuspecting of my deception, thinking only that I had hooked a fish so big that I was unable to raise its mighty head, nor even to wrest one solitary fin to the surface. Beads of sweat trickled down my forehead as I strove to make the battle look more convincing. It was nearly ten minutes since I had hooked this accursed hunk of rock and seen my chance to turn the tables on my tormentors. But things had got out of hand. I had not thought it through.

The game would soon be up. I cringed at the potential embarrassment.

Further down the bank, a slight movement caught my eye. Until then, I had been completely unaware of the wizened, stooped little man with the flat cap and the shapeless tweed jacket, fishing quietly just a few yards along the bank. His split cane rod sparkled as the sunlight caught the varnish, his creel sat on the bank by a clump of bullrushes and a thermos poked from his jacket pocket. In the split second it took me to register this vague impression, I realised that his arm was drawn back and his hand clutched a chunk of stone. Before I could react, the stone described a perfect arc across the water to land with a loud splash somewhere behind my tormentors.

To a man, the oncoming hordes jerked round. Seizing my chance, I lowered my rod until the tip pointed straight along the line and pulled with all my might. For the one and only time in my fishing life, I breathed a huge sigh of relief as the line and leader parted company and the line hurtled back towards me minus the weighted damsel nymph. Wasting not a moment, I reeled in, cursing loudly and heaving my shoulders in mock despair. The spell broken, my audience nodded sympathetically and turned back towards their own abandoned tackle.

Belatedly, I turned to peer back down the bank, feeling both grateful to my saviour and sheepish at the need for his intervention. There was no one in sight. A slight breath of wind ruffled the reeds and a little shadow ran across the grass, disappearing into the setting sun. But of my silent benefactor and his tackle, there was no sign.

That file was filling rapidly.

4

A TASTE FOR LIFE

My children are at the age when eating represents a diversion from much more important activities like whacking each other with plastic swords, jumping out from behind the kitchen door wielding light sabres or shadow kicking like karate black belts at the local gym. Food is necessary (so long as it isn't green or spicy) but only as a means to an end: refuelling the tank and keeping the parents quiet.

I assume I was no different when I was that age, except that my driving force was more likely to be football than *Men in Black*, *Star Wars* or their sixties equivalents. In common with so many parental commands, the requirement to remain at the table until everyone else had finished, struck me as needlessly authoritarian, completely pointless and a waste of valuable playing time to boot. Now that the shoe is firmly on the other foot, I struggle not to feel a certain degree of empathy with my children.

As a youngster fishing with my father, eating seemed an even more irritating and unnecessary constraint on my time than it did at home. Flies hooked in the cork handle of my trusty Greenheart were not about to engineer the downfall of the monster trout I firmly believed had my name tattooed boldly on its dorsal fin every time I ventured to the water's edge. My father's restlessness after just a couple of hours and his surreptitious glances at the picnic box were almost more than I could bear.

In keeping with my good Edinburgh upbringing, I was weaned unashamedly on a solid diet of home made broth, meat, potato and veg, with old-fashioned milk puddings for afters and porridge for breakfast. Spicy foreign foods were a wholly new experience that lay in wait when I became an impressionable student eager to spread my wings and experience life's variety. I had my first curry on Sauchiehall Street served by an immigrant Indian with an incongruously broad Glaswegian dialect and a Celtic shirt. I was instantly hooked.

I suspect that the lateness of my conversion to the delights of pseudo-Indian cuisine served only to strengthen in me the macho, pointless and potentially kamikaze urge to prove my masculinity in the curry house. For years, I am sure I gave all too many long-suffering Indian waiters that rare thrill which must brighten an otherwise monotonous existence: the brazen demand for the one dish described on the menu as 'extremely spicy', 'mind-blowing' or 'hotter than a vindaloo'. In other words, the selection that gives the cook *carte blanche* to empty an entire tin of curry powder and half a dozen chilli peppers into one sizzling dish without fear of reprisal. Of course, I regretted it every time, secretly resolved never to repeat the mistake, and went back out and did it all over again.

My newly acquired and somewhat lofty perspective on the joys of *haute cuisine* (reflected, incidentally, in some blessedly short-lived culinary adventures of my own) had a profound impact on my waterside lunchbox. Gone was the white bread hastily spread with margarine, processed cheese stuffed haphazardly between slices. In its place, a wedge of best stilton, a hunk of crusty brown loaf, savoury biscuits individually wrapped in cling film and a handful of grapes (seedless, of course).

For convenience, sandwiches remained the staple but tuna, mayonnaise and sweetcorn was the favourite filling, along with bacon (crisped nicely and frequently combined with a thin layer of cream cheese to offset the salty flavour). A nice slice of honey-roast ham was a regular contender, vying with grilled sausage, sometimes even a sliver of smoked salmon and a few home made oatcakes.

Then there were the 'sweet meats' from the delicatessen counter, where I spent Friday evenings standing in line clutching my numbered ticket. Satay sticks, perhaps, with a little carton of satay sauce, or a couple of onion bhajis to spice up the morning coffee break, a slab of pork and apple pie for later on. I did not quite stretch to the tablecloth, napkins and chilled Chablis but, for all that, the contents of my Waitrose carrier bag would not have looked out of place at Henley or Royal Ascot.

Of course, in the end, practicality and my Scottish disdain for soft southern habits won the day. Slicing cheeses and dipping satay sticks with hands devoid of all feeling is not easy while sitting in the driver's seat balancing a mug of coffee on one knee and simultaneously bracing oneself against successive blasts from a near gale force wind.

So, with time, I have rationalised somewhat, reducing the extravagance to a more manageable level. But I do still accord a degree of care and thought to the contents of the lunch box even now, when time is at such a premium. On a bad day, a tasty lunch can add a bit of colour to the proceedings and genuinely lift the spirits. You would be amazed at how often the first fish of the day has followed within minutes of a satisfying lunch break. Perhaps the effect is psychological; perhaps it is just that a break forces the angler to take stock. It is amazing what you can miss when you are concentrating.

Fishing is, for the most part, a solitary occupation. Yet, on a fine day, when the weather is benign and the company good, there is a tremendous degree of pleasure to be had in lunchtime banter. Were it not for such occasions, the whole fishing experience would be much the poorer and I, certainly, would have less to write about.

So, although I have not quite plumbed the depths to which my father sank (given half a chance, he would happily devour both my lunch and his before even casting a line), lunch has taken its rightful place as a focal point in my angling day. It provides welcome punctuation to the unfolding chapter, giving the whole experience a symmetry that would otherwise be missing.

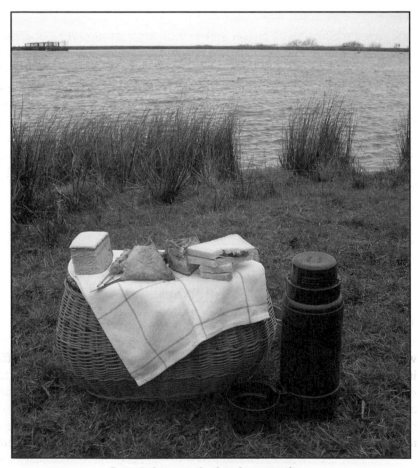

Lunchtime on the local reservoir

5

MONTANA MUSINGS

L ine fairly sizzled through the rod rings as the fish continued, effortlessly, to make deep inroads into my backing for the second time in as many minutes. Wild exhilaration mingled with panic as I tried clumsily to check this latest assertion of the trout's dominance, all fingers and thumbs struggling to adjust to the left-fixed (American-style) reel. Impossibly far away, my leader cut through the water at an alarming rate, causing the little float to bob up and down like a demented animal on a leash. In a tense voice, I urged Joe to get back on the oars. I need not have bothered; our guide had anticipated my needs and was already bending his back with purpose.

This was fishing like I had never done it before: fishing Montana-style. The rig (cast to you and me) comprised a little luminescent bite indicator (float) which could be moved up and down the leader with the minimum of effort in response to changing depth and feeding behaviour, and a team of tiny weighted nymphs. This combination did not make for easy casting, especially with a strong wind blowing unabated across the open, summer-dry plains directly into our faces; so much so that, on occasion, Joe was forced to row downstream just to stop us from ending up back where we had started.

The boat itself was a veritable Rolls Royce, designed to make the angler comfortable beyond his wildest dreams: padded swivel seat, waterproof storage compartments (hey, where's the fun in dry sandwiches?) and safety rails to enable the fisher to cast from a standing position in complete safety. But therein lies the secret of American life: when our trans-Atlantic relatives do something, they do it properly, be it burgers, political scandals or fishing boats.

Behind me, hunched over the oars, ruddy face aglow with a combination of weather and pride, our guide did the real work, uncomplaining, keeping the boat rock-steady with quiet skill and bluff good humour.

As if to act as a counterpoint to the cool sophistication and high technology of our floating palace, the Missouri herself showered natural wonders upon us, like gifts, around every new corner. The elegant magnificence of a soaring bald eagle riding the winds and the lethal grace of a fishing osprey intent on providing for a growing clutch, contrasted with the comical inquisitiveness of a muskrat regarding us through intelligent eyes and a fringe of damp whiskers.

All these things Joe pointed out, while somehow continuing to keep a close eye on our bite indicators, casually declaring even the merest of dips in the little floats when our attention wandered unforgivably. In quiet moments, he imparted gems of wisdom accumulated over seasons of meticulous guiding, or related tales to feed the imagination and bolster the confidence to the point at which every cast promised the fish of a lifetime.

In just a day, as we drifted from one 'hole' to the next, I learned more about fishing than I had done for a very long time. I learnt by watching the progress of the little float, how even the minutest drag could spook the biggest and boldest of rainbows. And I learnt too, just how gentle the take of a nymphing trout could be, how the tiny morsel could be sucked in delicately and rejected with only the merest dip of the float by way of indication. How many times over the years, without the benefit of such simple technology, had I been blissfully unaware of missed chances? Best left to the imagination, perhaps …

The fish was tiring and the battle nearly won.

The boat drifted freely now as Joe abandoned the oars and reached for the net. My wife fumbled excitedly with the camera. Wrist aching and heart pounding, only Old Man River seemed unconcerned: he, at least, had

Above: **The evening rise begins on a Montana 'pond'**
Below: **Into another good rainbow on the Missouri**

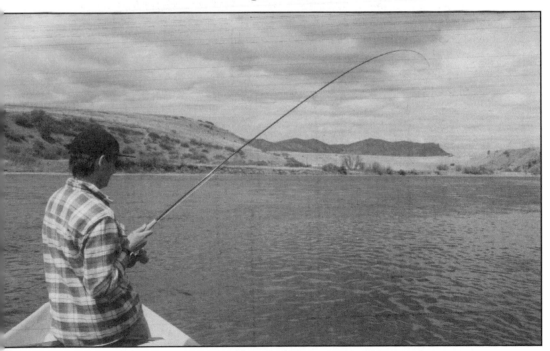

seen it all before.

Then, all in a rush, the relief, the pride, the smiles, the congratulations, the moment of quiet wonder … and finally, the careful return of the river's own.

A fitting climax to a memorable experience: the trip of a lifetime for us to a bewitching place up in the mountains surrounded only by nature and silence. What a wonderful country! Big, wild rainbows, full-finned and glinting scales, wily, deep-bellied brown trout, lively, cutthroat in pretty mountain creeks, and dashing brook trout, all spotted flanks and white-embroidered fins. Where else could the angler encounter such variety? Where else did so many members of the salmonid family take a seat at the same table with equanimity?

And now? Ah well, now it is back to reality: the pressures of work, the family squabbles, the wet weekends and, perhaps, if I'm lucky, a hard boat seat, aching arms, a cold bailing can and wet sandwiches.

Chalk and cheese, really!

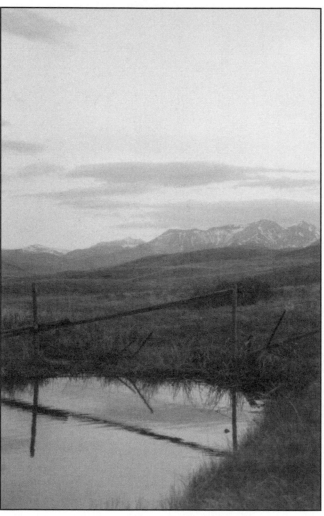

A quiet corner on a Montana lake

PART XI
LIFE BEGINS AT FORTY

Just another number, they said, but they were wrong.

All of a sudden, life seemed a touch ephemeral, as if, somewhere, a celestial contract had been drawn up, complete with an end date. Cherished dreams and ambitions, some barely conscious, were slipping through the fingers with alarming speed. It was a time for quiet acceptance or determined defiance: there could be no half-way house.

Yet, bafflingly, my own perception of myself remained unchanged. In my mind, I was still the same person with the same thoughts, the same feelings, the same ambitions that had been mine twenty years before. Still the brave idealist at work, the fun-loving, sports-mad 'youngster' outside. But when the millennium streamers had turned to pulp in the grey January rain and the champagne had lost its sparkle, the next century would belong to my children and to their children. It would be their turn to strive to make a difference, mine to watch from an armchair.

So forty was a milestone: a milestone on a road that flashed by with growing speed. And, in truth, I felt just a little helpless: the passenger, someone else's foot on the accelerator.

1

THE LATE SHIFT

B y the time they reach forty, 82% of men are married, including 93% of those who swore they would never tread the aisle. If you assume that single men spend 60% of their time directly or indirectly trying to find a mate (a conservative assumption based on my experience), that should leave an awful lot of forty-something men with an awful lot of time on their hands.

So why are we always so busy? Well, there is the decorating to do, the grass to cut, the homework to check, the overtime to put in, the car to clean. All this hype about increased leisure time is just that: a falsehood generated and actively encouraged by those who have leisure services to sell. As every day passes, my leisure time diminishes at about the same rate as the energy I have left to put it to good use. Sometimes, even fishing seems like an effort.

But of course, or so they tell us, married men have a much more exciting lifestyle these days than ever before. Let's just look at that assertion a little more closely, shall we?

As a single man, you spent your time with (or tried to spend your time with) single women. The reward, on those rare occasions you breached the inner defences, was a glimpse of something exciting and not entirely understood. Lacy underwear drying on the radiator, high heeled shoes spilling from the wardrobe, frilly pillow slips and flimsy night-dresses. In short, a very different world to the one you were used to: your own bachelor pad, with its stale odours, dirty washing and dusty shelves decorated with foreign beer bottles and photos of dead trout.

As a forty-something married man, what has replaced this? Well, for a start, lace is out. Underwear is purely functional, designed to cover everything from mid-thigh to neck. Gone are the beer bottles and the photos, long since consigned to the recycling bin or that box under the stair which you refuse to part with.

Now I am not saying that married life is without its attractions. Nor am I saying that the older woman can't be sexy. You have only to look at Jenny Agutter, Helen Mirren or Gemma Craven to scotch any doubts on this count. But it takes a bit more effort and that, in turn, means that it takes time. The latter, of course, is in short supply unless the lady in question happens to be an ageing actress with a driver, butler, wardrobe mistress and healthy bank balance.

In recognition of the changing age profile of Britain's population, the TV programme makers have gone overboard on gardening, relocation and DIY. There can be little doubt these extravaganzas are aimed at us. The star presenters employed with such carefree abandon, assume that we would rather spend our precious spare time constructing patios than fishing, that our children never kick a football and that our neighbours relish the prospect of the rear view of a Japanese pagoda. Our living rooms are turned into palaces of MDF festooned with candles and billowing hangings that, in my house at least, would have Spiderman ensnared in their delicate folds before you could say Laurence Llewelyn-Bowen.

Of course, the key elements of all this, to return pretty much to where we started, are time and money. About the only things that used to keep me sane in life were my forward taper floating line, Tups Indispensible and Richard Walker 'Little Lake'. These days, the opportunity to salvage my sanity by indulging in fishing, or any other solitary pastime which fails to contribute in any practical sense to the running of the household, is rare to the point of imminent extinction.

Indeed, fishing during daylight hours is fast becoming about as likely as Scotland scoring twice at the correct end.

Which explains why I found myself on Inchy Bridge at 2100 hours one August evening sharing the 'craic' with a band of like-minded Irishmen in sheer defiance of my normal ambition for this sort of hour, namely, a bottle of wine, a good book and the prospect of a few hours of peaceful slumber. However, with the fly rod still to see any meaningful action that season, no self-respecting angler could have resisted for long the temptation of such a fine little river. After all, what did next week have in store but a bathroom to redecorate and an office full of accumulated paperwork?

This time, I was determined not to repeat the mistakes of my last night-time foray. On that occasion, I had dithered too long by the bridge, soaking up the atmosphere while the regulars exchanged gentle conversation and river watched. By the time I had reached my allotted pool, the last vestiges of light had long since disappeared. Fishing a pool at night without first walking it during daylight hours is not an experience I would recommend. Three hours later, I had trudged wearily home, mud spattered, fishless and with a fly box terminally impoverished after numerous skirmishes with the devilishly obstructive bankside vegetation.

So tonight I had determined to get there with ample time to observe the pool in the waning light of dusk and measure the distances in my mind's eye, even, perhaps, to try a few casts while there was still enough light to appreciate the perspectives. Should I hook a fish, I would hand-line him in to avoid the necessity of working out afresh how much line I could safely cast. Most of all, I was determined to stay alert and not to react as sluggishly as I had done last time a fish had responded to my increasingly frantic efforts.

As I stood a yard or so back from the bank, waiting quietly for the light to wane just enough for the stream bed to fade from sight, I felt my senses heighten. Every small sound from the dense bramble-laden undergrowth seemed magnified in the stillness: the eerie screech of foraging fox, the soft whoosh of ghostly feathers as an owl launched itself into the sky to begin a night of hunting, the whirr and splash as the first sea trout leapt, performing a flamboyant tail stand on the quiet surface of the pool.

It was time. As I began to lengthen my line, my heart thumped against my ribcage and my eyes ached from peering into the deepening gloom. One cast, two casts, three casts. Suddenly, a flurry of froth no more than six feet from where I stood. An arm wrenching strain on the rod. Sheer mayhem as a good sea trout made off down river, shattering the starry reflections in a series of breathtaking leaps.

Please God, just this one fish, let him be hooked! The runs got gradually shorter. I fumbled briefly with the net. Careful. Resist the temptation to lunge at shadows. Keep his head up and draw him in firmly. Raise the net. Got him!

I collapsed on the bank in a heap, elation coursing through my veins. Two pounds of burnished silver shimmered in the moonlight, every fin and spot perfect. My first night-time sea trout.

Two hours later, I had four, all taken within scant yards of each other. I lost just one. Far above the darkness of the treetops, a shooting star illuminated the sky briefly, a celestial firework set off in celebration of a good night's work. Following the slender beam of the torchlight, I threaded my way back along the narrow path, through the bramble thickets, careful as

I passed the dense stands of nettles, heavy from a summer's growth. Just in time, I remembered to duck to avoid the overhanging hawthorn branches clawing at my face in the darkness. Finally, back to the bridge to share the glories of a fine evening in hushed, reverential whispers by the glowing light of cigarette.

A little later, as I returned to the cottage along the narrow winding road, breathing in the strong smell of seaweed through the open car window, I pondered idly on family life and the hectic pace of a modern existence. If only I could bottle that little river and the timeless part of the past in which it nestled, and take it home with me across the Irish Sea. Then, perhaps, the strains of middle age might seem more bearable.

The author's first night-time sea trout, Argideen, Eire

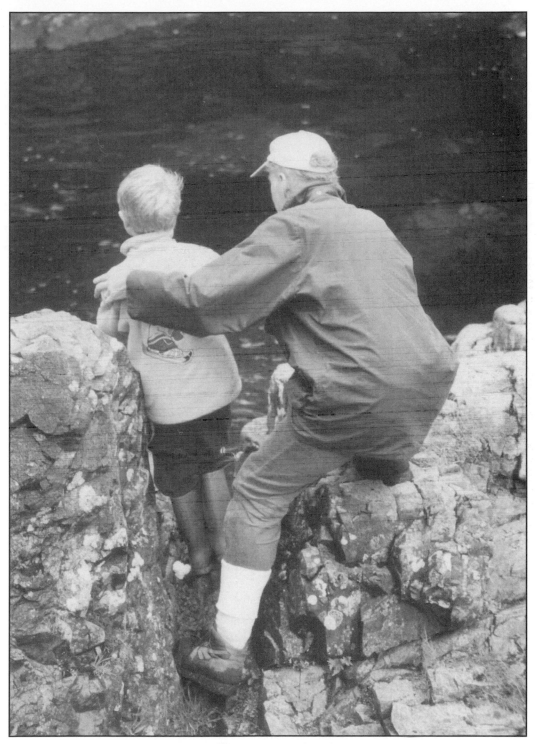

Like father, like son: scanning the depths

2

OLD DOGS
AND NEW TRICKS

I have to admit, I had never really subscribed to the recognised wisdom. Until recently, that is. Then, in the interests of that quaint little concept called personal development, my boss persuaded me to attend a study course on radiological protection: stochastic risks, transmission curves and antiparticles, positrons, kermas, Bremsstrahlung, DDREFs, RBEs and LETs.

Suffice it to say that within half an hour of Day One my mind had strayed abstractedly to truly weighty problems: like how to catch the trout which repeatedly splashes at your deer-hair sedge but refuses to take hold or persuading the painter to come back and finish the exterior job he started last summer.

As it happens, I had barely resolved the problem of the recalcitrant trout, when I was jogged from my comfortable state of catatonia by the arrival on the podium of the gorgeous Dr Easterbrook, sweeping dramatically into the lecture theatre amid a cloud of perfume, all painted nails, peroxide blonde hair and 6 inch heels, a stark and bewitching contrast to the faintly crumpled tweeds and tartan tie of her predecessor. One flash of stocking tops and I was agog for the duration of 'standards and units', all thoughts of painters and warm afternoons by the waterside temporarily forgotten.

If I remember nothing else from these three days, which in all probability I will not, at least the definition of 'Sievert' is indelibly stamped on my memory and I can tell you without hesitation, how to convert equivalent dose into effective dose. Five out of five on the post-course assessment form, no question.

But as the day trundled on and the heady excitement of 'standards and units' faded to a distant memory, a feeling of disquiet grew and blossomed: a feeling that all around me those fresh-faced and serious-looking youngsters were understanding, learning and, what was worse, evidently enjoying the experience. When seven o'clock and the close of the first day finally arrived, all I wanted was a pint and a quiet stroll down to the little chalk stream meandering peacefully through the village by the hotel. My colleagues, or so it seemed, could hardly wait to get back to their rooms, plot a few decay curves, calculate some cost benefits and get stuck into a risk assessment or two.

Now please do not get me wrong, I do not have anything against the pursuit of knowledge. It is just that, by the time you've clocked up four decades, I like to think you are old enough and wise enough to save your attention for occasions where there is a sufficiently good reason (long legs and stocking tops being one such, pernickety trout being another). Chances are, for very good biological and behavioural reasons (not to mention toxicological ones) your brain cell count has entered the red zone and the warning light has started to flash. Even if you began life's journey with an IQ in excess of 160 (and therefore probably still have more brain cells than I had in my prime), the youthful zest for knowledge has faded somewhat.

And then you start to wonder whether, in fact, you were ever actually that serious about learning. Even in these far off student days, I honestly do not recall learning ranking very high on my list of priorities. From memory, reading *New Scientist* came somewhere around number twenty-eight, sandwiched uncomfortably between ironing and cooking (and only if I had a few minutes to spare before Not the Nine O'Clock News or my shift pulling pints behind the Athletic Club bar). Lectures were things to be attended selectively. In other words, when the subject matter was guaranteed to come up in the end of session exam, when your attendance record was in danger of being rumbled and when the close season ruled out any possibility of a quick cast. Yet I suspect my career has not suffered markedly as a result.

In much the same way, all these avidly devoured fishing magazines with their exotic flies, alien techniques and fancy equipment have never made much noticeable difference to my angling performance. Come to think about it, their only material impact has been to bolster my confidence for a time at least and provide the hope of better things in a piscatorial existence where the biggest catch would probably not inspire Bob Church to leave the comfort of his bedroom, never mind tackle up and wet a line in anger.

But to return to my recent learning experience, I did actually pass the post-course exam, thanks largely to an unblemished performance in 'standards and units'. Flushed by this success, I went straight out and bought myself a fishing video which offered to take the mystique out of small lake fishing.

Some hours later, having watched Simon Gawesworth explain in admirably simple terms how to splice a fly line to its backing, a task which usually leaves me with glue everywhere and a substantially shortened 'business end', and gawped in wonder as the narrator nonchalantly hooked a fine rainbow first cast with a Diawl Bach fished just sub-surface, followed by another on a dry fly and a third with a deep Montana, I could not help wondering where I had gone wrong all these years. You got the distinct impression that a meat pie attached to the end of the line would have been greeted with equal alacrity.

Undaunted, I tried the Gawesworth approach myself, in similar conditions, at the first opportunity. I will not dignify this little experiment by spelling out the results. Suffice it to say, this was when I finally began to suspect that there might just be something in the old saying.

After all, everything has its place in this life. With age, comes a certain wisdom: an acceptance of the truism that the more you learn, the less you know. Which, inevitably, takes a bit of the urgency out of learning it in the first place.

3

NEW-FANGLED
TECHNOLOGY

If you want to find out about angling clubs or buy tackle, it said in my fishing magazine, the Internet is for you. Excuse my scepticism. I am afraid I don't buy the theory that the world of electronic communication is there to make our lives easier or to give us the spare time we crave. For me, the language of the computer is about as comprehensible as one of Gordon Brown's budget day speeches, which is probably why I cling forlornly to the increasingly untenable belief that the telephone book is more efficient, necessary and accessible than the computer terminal (hence, emulating the brave but ultimately very wet, King Canute). It probably also explains my surprise at the recent discovery that 'IT' does not, in fact, stand for 'ideological trauma' as I had long believed it did.

Never mind the mysteries of the Net, I'm still trying to work out where the punch card comes out (after you feed it into the slot marked A-drive, that is). If such concerns periodically bring you out in a cold flush and leave you with an uneasy feeling of inadequacy, I can offer at least some consolation: this is not a gross deficiency in your genetic make-up. If you don't believe me, try a controlled experiment. Take a four-year-old who has never used a computer (a bit like trying to find a virgin in a brothel these days but it can be done), add a terminal, a key pad and a mouse (the electronic variety, not the cute furry one with whiskers). Next, point to a symbol on the screen (anything will do) and, at the risk of mixing rodents, instruct your guinea pig to 'put the mouse there'.

Without hesitation and without any show of embarrassment, I can guarantee that your four-year-old will respond instantly by lifting the mouse from the mat and physically placing it on the screen. (I actually repeated the experiment a couple of times just to make myself feel better). Of course, the down side is that two years later, the same youngster will be decapitating hideous monsters at level 3 of 'Intergalactic Heroes' while you are still trying to get the space ship off the launch pad.

To try to rationalise my inadequacies, I have developed this theory that IT is actually just a mind set. The baffling terminology is a subtle smoke screen devised to throw you off the scent, to baffle and frustrate, to preserve the mystique for those paid lots more than you to be experts. Bytes and rams, download and boot up, modems and disc drives – they're all part of the facade.

Have you ever had that dreadful experience in your local computer megastore (why is a technology based on the 'micro' chip invariably referred to as 'mega', incidentally?) when the pimply youth with the Doc Martens and the earring through one or other fleshy region looks at you with that barely concealed mixture of pity and frustration, and starts talking extremely slowly as if the act of repeating the same indecipherable words at half the pace will somehow make them immediately understandable?

But to return to my waterlogged surfboard and my stuttering search for angling wisdom on the e-waves, 'carbon fibre rods' took me to an industrial site in West Virginia which manufactured intermediate products for the automobile trade. 'Landing net' led to a fascinating virtual tour of a company selling airfield hardware, while 'rubber products' rewarded me with an interesting and educational half hour and the rough edge of my wife's tongue but no discernible information on the price of thigh waders. And they say you travel fast on the electronic highway.

You might think that the act of fishing itself could be expected to remain largely unsullied by technology. After all, fishing is an ancient pastime, a tradition rich in taboos and conservatism. You would, of course, be wrong. A brief perusal of the mail order catalogues (which, needless to say, encourage us to order 'on the web') is instant proof that things have moved on since the days of horse-hair leaders. Fluorocarbon, braided loops and copolymer leaders turn the process of tying your fly to your line into a technological adventure of epic proportions.

When my fingers were nimble enough and my eyesight good enough to dabble in a bit of fly tying, a few feathers from the hackle of some unfortunate farmyard hen, a couple of hooks, some thread, wax, a vice and infinite patience were about all you needed. Nowadays, any fly tier worth his salt has a cabinet the size of a small wardrobe stuffed with everything from rabbit zonkers to llama mix, krystal flash and holographic tinsel.

Not long ago, I came across an old Hardy palakona rod gathering dust on a shelf in the conservatory of my mother's house. The varnish was peeling in places and a few of the rings were bent but, all told, the rod was in remarkably good condition for its age. I assembled it and felt for the first time in many years the unique balance of a good split cane rod. Before I knew it, I found kindled within me a desire to return to the simple things, a bit like the participants whisked from a normal twenty-first century existence and asked to survive in log cabins on the prairie or circumnavigate the globe in a life-size replica of Charles Darwin's Beagle, all for the sake of TV entertainment.

So I took the rod to be restored and found a basket weaver at a local craft fair to make me an old fashioned creel. Now, as long as I have my twenty-first century car to get me there, my Gore-Tex waders to keep me dry and my Ultra-3 floating line (with advanced hydrophobic chemistry and Microballoon technology) to maximise my catching potential, I can at least pretend to be following in the footsteps of Izaak Walton himself.

I suspect, however, that the great man may turn in his grave at the very thought.

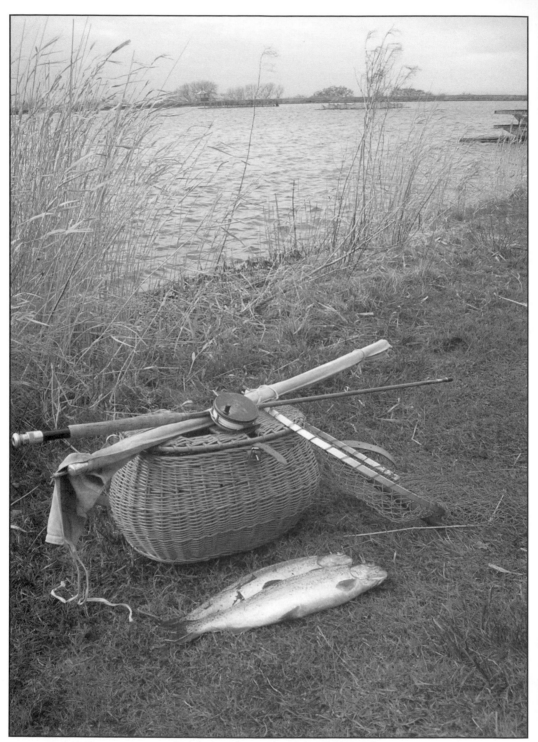

Just to prove the old ways can be best

4

THE DAY
IS WHAT YOU SEE

Unbidden, the lyrics of Uist men and contemporary songwriters, Calum and Rory Macdonald, drifted through my consciousness:

> The sun is melting over the hills
> All our roads are waiting
> To be revealed
> For this day in history
> Has brought us to here
> Now it's all there for the taking
> The day is what you see*

A lot had happened since last I was here. Nelson Mandela had walked free. The Berlin Wall had fallen. The Scottish Parliament had passed from dream to reality. I had seen seven years at University, made a career, bought and sold three houses, become a family, lost a father, lived nearly half a lifetime.

However I might see myself, I had changed: I was older, more resigned, less naïve. Yet this place had been the same since the beginning of time. In my head, childhood memories crowded around the sweeping lyrics of the Macdonalds' song. Above me, the mountains gently mocked my limited human perspective. Below me, the loch smiled beguilingly, beckoning me down to her delicately reed-fringed shores, gentle yet insistent, enticing me to cool my brow with her sparkling water, urging me to cast a line and to sample her bounty. A siren from ancient mythology.

As I strode nearer through the springy summer heather, I saw for just a moment the bare, tanned head of my father bobbing in front, stride lengthening in anticipation, leading me on in silent companionship.

I got there at last and on her shores I sat for a while, lost in thought, wondering at the ease with which the years had slipped past, shocked by a potent realisation of the triviality of all that seemed so important. In the end, I dragged myself from my reveries with a conscious effort and put up a rod, suddenly impatient to concentrate on the present.

The fish that came to my net were not large. But they were as I remembered them. Hard fighting, pretty little fish, flanks spotted in cheerful yellows and reds, bellies sparkling silver in the sunshine. I took enough for dinner and no more. I felt that this was the best way to honour my hostess' generosity and her gracious tolerance of this unasked for intrusion.

I looked back once as I began the hike home. The sun, dipping now towards the ridge, sparkled briefly off the water, the loch bidding me a coquettish farewell. I wondered whether I would ever return. If I did, how would the world look then? Where would life have taken me?

Questions I could not answer. I realised that I knew with certainty but two things. That this place would be the same. And that I fervently hoped I would return.

*Lyrics from Runrig song, *Maymorning*, reproduced by kind permission of Chrysalis and the band.

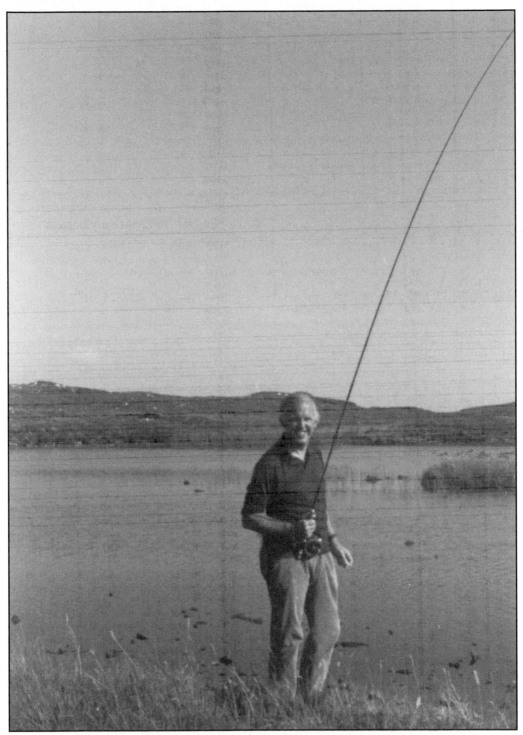

The simple pleasures: the author's father on one of his beloved hill lochs

Epilogue

We may say of angling, as Dr. Boteley said of strawberries, 'Doubtless God could have made a better berry, but doubtless God never did,' and so, if I might judge, God never did make a more calm, quiet, innocent recreation than angling.

Izaak Walton

In the end, curiosity, nostalgia and patriotism got the better of me. I went last night to see that quintessentially Scottish band, Runrig, perform in Liverpool. Before the gig, I stood awhile in a Scouse pub awash with ghosts from a Scottish past. Harsh Glaswegian accents mixed easily with the gentle lilt of the Isles. Briefly, I was transported back to the little, smoky night-club on Sauchiehall Street where I first heard the band, surrounded by madly gyrating students oozing vitality and optimism for the future. Not for the first time in recent months, I wondered where it had all gone.

They say it happens to everyone. One night you go to bed as usual, the next morning you waken to the realisation that this is it, this is as good as it gets. You will never go clubbing with Kylie, fire the Head of Human Resources, catch monster salmon on the Kharlovka or watch Scotland win the World Cup in the Marracana. Psychologists call it the mid-life crisis, except that, for me, it was more of a nagging worry than a crisis.

When it comes down to it, I am no different to most middle-aged anglers. Life and fishing revolve around a few key facts: wife, children, job, mortgage and car (two, in my case – the price paid to keep the wife working, a necessary consequence of the children and the mortgage). The stark realisation that I find myself struggling to adjust to is that after half a lifetime of job applications and house moves, in all probability I am stuck with my current lot for the rest of my working days. I am trapped, like so many other working men: mortgages, loans and student fees for sums not yet imaginable depend on my diligently bartering my days for pounds. Short of staging a disappearing act reminiscent of Reggie Perrin (and, believe me, I have no compelling desire to enter the water in the vicinity of Blackpool Pleasure Beach with or without my underpants) I have no other option.

If I am to maintain my family's modest lifestyle, I am destined to continue setting out for the office at 0730 hours just as I have done for years, attend stressful meetings discussing subjects whose importance in the scheme of things I have long since ceased to grasp, eat a sandwich lunch at my desk and return home at 1800 hours after forty-five minutes stuck in ever-worsening traffic jams, only to find the children arguing like cat and dog, and my wife on the point of strangling them (or me, as murdering one's husband is generally considered to be a less heinous crime than killing one's children).

Perhaps that is why I have started having these recurring dreams: dreams in which stockings and handcuffs feature large. Quite natural at my age, you might say. The only thing is that the stockings are on the head and the handcuffs dangle at the waist of a brawny security guard. You see, the dream is about the ultimate heist, the robbery to end all robberies. No violence, just one sure, clean raid. In and out with no clues left, only some faceless, nameless financial institute loses out. No greed, no repeat performance, just enough money to stop working and move the family to that cabin with the trout river and the veranda.

If I had a pound for each time I have been asked why I fish, I would be a wealthy man indeed. And, if the truth be known, I have asked myself the same question more often than you might imagine. Over the years, I have been attacked by the flailing hooves of semi-wild horses, eaten alive by midges, stung by wasps, drenched to the skin, frozen and sunburnt. Yet on the flip side I have watched otters play, ospreys hunt and beavers forage, sights denied to most in this fleeting life we live. Along the way, just occasionally, I have even managed to catch a fish or two.

It is my fervent hope that these experiences, pleasures and tribulations alike, will endure for future generations to savour; I believe that through them my life has been enriched beyond measure.

And yet, when I stop to examine my motivations closely, there is still more to this fishing game. Fishing is in my blood. When I see water, I think fish, just as others see mountains and think of the top. For me, fishing is like a steadying anchor in the midst of life's turmoil. When I want peace, when I want solitude to contemplate or to forget, I take to the water. And such is the beauty of fishing that when I need the opposite, when I hunger for the cheerful companionship of endeavours shared, fishing can provide that too.

Perhaps that is why the hills are my real spiritual home. The contrasting qualities of companionship on the long walk out and solitude as I fish round the bank, all the time absorbed by the unfolding secrets of a new loch, treading perhaps, where no other has tread since the beginning of time.

These are the pleasures I value most and the reason why I have never felt at home on the small stock ponds which abound where I now live. The fish might be large and the fishing challenging but I do not want to be shoulder to shoulder with my fellow angler all day, nor to be confined by his pace of fishing, or to catch stock fish, predictable in their size and lethargy. Instead, I want to cover new water with every step, not knowing whether the next fish will be big or small, wondering what spectacle might greet my inquisitive gaze around each point. When I return from such a day, no matter the weather or the catch, I return purged, temporarily at least, of the pressures and stresses of modern existence.

Fishing on the local 'stock' pond !

Perhaps too, the gentle philosophy of my fishing mentors has influenced my own life and standards: my father's simple pleasure in the countryside, Mr Doull's gentle humour and unfailing courtesy, my maths teacher's jovial perseverance and optimism. All were individuals, as different as chalk and cheese, yet each was (or is) a gentleman in a timeless manner unfashionable in today's 'speak your mind' society.

I want to reach my twilight years with stories to tell over a whisky by the fire, stories to excite and entertain my companions, stories told with a twinkle in the eye to belie the advancing years. I want to be remembered with a gentle smile playing on the lips. What worse fate than for life to squeeze you dry, to leave a husk empty of humour with only relief to mark its passing. Perhaps these are modest ambitions, redolent of a less materialistic age, but if I succeed in achieving them, then I suspect I will be a happier and richer man than most.

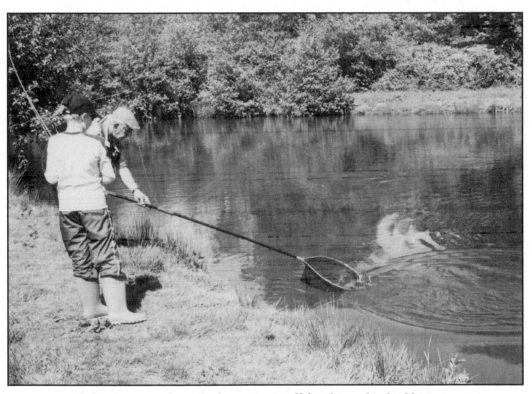

A day to remember: the lessons pay off for the author's eldest son